Business Model Design and Learning

Business Model Design and Learning

A Strategic Guide

Barbara Spencer

businessexpert
Press

First published in 2013 by
Business Expert Press, LLC
222 East 46th Street, New York, NY 10017
www.businessexpertpress.com

ISBN-13: 978-1-60649-486-8 (paperback)

ISBN-13: 978-1-60649-487-5 (e-book)

DOI 10.4128/9781606494875

Business Expert Press Strategic Management collection

Collection ISSN: 2150-9611 (print)
Collection ISSN: 2150-9646 (electronic)

Cover design and interior design by Exeter Premedia Services Private Ltd., Chennai, India

First edition: 2013

10 9 8 7 6 5 4 3 2 1

Printed in the United States of America.

With assistance from R. Kellon Lawrence

Abstract

The purpose of this book is to explain what a business model is, what you have to do to get one, and what to do about the one you've already got. It contends that to be successful, your business model must be focused sharply on your customer. And it argues that you must think strategically about how to use your business model if you want to gain an advantage over your competitors.

This book is aimed at aspiring entrepreneurs and practicing managers who want to create new business models as well as managers and leaders who want to understand, refine, and even reinvent their company's current model. It is based on the premise that the fundamental purpose of any business model is to create, deliver, and capture value. More specifically, business models describe the value proposition to the customer, the system that must be in place to create that value, and the logics needed to capture a reasonable share of that value for the firm. In addition, the book shows that the core of every business model is an agreement with your customers. If they don't get the value they are seeking, you won't either.

The book proceeds as follows. First, it clearly defines business models and explains how they relate to strategy. Second, it presents seven basic components of business models, including the customer value proposition, key resources, key processes, the profit formula, the aspirations and capabilities of key leaders, the customers and the customer relationships. These components are then combined into three business model lenses which can be used to explain how a business creates and captures value. As the book proceeds, these three business model lenses are used to explore the value creating capabilities of several companies including Bomgar, TOMS Shoes, Netflix, Rent-the-Runway, and J.C. Penney. Each story provides lessons and implications related to effective business modeling and strategy.

Keywords

business model, business model components, business model lenses, customer value proposition, value appropriation, profit formula, target customer, customer perceived value, customer value agreement, customer value relationship, business model experimentation, business modeling

Contents

Chapter 1   Why Business Models Matter..1

Chapter 2   Three Business Model Lenses 13

Chapter 3   How the Bomgar Box Delivers
Customer Value 27

Chapter 4   A Ham Radio Company Builds a Superior
Business Model 39

Chapter 5   TOMS Shoes: Selling a Vision 49

Chapter 6   Netflix Cancels the Value Exchange Agreement............61

Chapter 7   Rent the Runway: Changing Customer
Behaviors and Industry Norms.....................................69

Chapter 8   J.C. Penney's Big Experiment 79

Chapter 9   Ten Key Ideas About Business Models 93

Appendix A: Pricing Mechanisms 105

Appendix B: Online Marketplaces 115

Notes...119

References 127

Index 135

CHAPTER 1

Why Business Models Matter

Recently, I flew home from Canada after attending a conference. As a relatively frequent flyer, I was happy to be upgraded to first class and as my flight was at noontime, I was looking forward to a nice meal on a white tablecloth. To my surprise, on a two-hour flight, all I got was a beverage and some peanuts. When we landed, I found that my luggage had not arrived. As I waited in line to fill out the paperwork, I was not a happy camper.

Why is it that flying anywhere so often turns out to be a frustrating experience? In his blog, Patrick Stähler contends that the airlines are facing problems because their business model is broken.[1] Neither the customers nor the firms are receiving the value they seek. He reports that in the years following 2000, the average airline generated an EBIT margin of just 0.7% while thousands of passengers posted their disgruntled stories online.

According to Stähler, airlines have created this state of affairs by training their customers to search multiple channels for the lowest possible price, regardless of the fact that the experience that comes with such a price is likely to be unsatisfactory.[2] We customers play along because we know that prices go up and down, and because we have the power to search out good deals on the Internet. Indeed, we feel taken when we find that a better price was available on a different website, or at a later date. We've continued to play along even though we've had to forgo our free meals, squeeze into ever smaller seats, and carry on our bags to avoid fees for checking in our luggage. And just as we learned to put all of our one-ounce cosmetics containers into one-quart plastic bags, we faced new charges for carry-on luggage. Each change feels like a kick in the teeth. They were not part of the bargain. We feel ripped off. Our experience of value has deteriorated.

In this case, neither the customers nor the airlines are satisfied with the value they are receiving. In contrast, a successful business model is based on an agreement between a company and its customers—an agreement that all parties will get what they need. It is an agreement about the fair exchange of value that should take place when two parties do business together. This agreement may not be stated out loud or written clearly, but it frames our expectations and reactions. When it is violated, customers become angry, firms lose profitability, and industries spiral downward. In the airline example, both the firms and the customers are dissatisfied with the value they are receiving. It may be time for a new model.

Stähler contends that the airlines have focused too much on keeping up with their competitors and too little on their relationship with their customers.[3] They have allowed their product to be defined as a commodity as opposed to exploring new pricing models and sensible alternatives. To put it another way, they have focused too much on strategy and not enough on providing customer value. As a result the customer relationship has become increasingly hostile, while internal changes have continued to focus on cutting costs, reducing seat sizes, and adding new charges for luggage and food. Real change will require dialogue with customers and explicit examination of tacitly held assumptions. Or it will come from an upstart with a new way of looking at things.

The purpose of this book is to explain what a business model is, what you have to do to get one, and what to do about the one you've already got. I will argue strongly that your business model must be focused on your customer—like a laser—if you are going to be successful. And that you have to think strategically about how to use your business model to gain an advantage over your competitors. It's a dog eat dog world. Customers have lots of choices.

On the other hand, I believe that this is a great time to go into business. Gaining access to customers, while still tough, is easier than ever before; new online marketplaces allow you to sell your products right beside the big guys. And there are many new ways to price your services and get paid for your work: from subscriptions, to paywalls, to Paypal. You can even swipe credit cards on your iPhone.

This book is written both for people who may want to start a business and for those who work for one and want to make it better. People in both situations have much to gain by clarifying their understanding of business models and putting that knowledge to work.

In the next section, I will explain what a business model is and what it isn't. I will talk about the differences between business models and strategy, and the relationships between business models and strategy. Finally, I will explain what it means to think strategically about your business model.

What Is a Business Model?

A business model is a tool or a framework that can assist you in figuring out how you can use what you've got to make something of value for a customer while making money for yourself.[4] It is the way a system of activities comes together to create a product or service offering and deliver it to the customer. A good business model clearly explains the core logic behind the system, how it all works together to create and capture value.[5]

Every business model is framed around a customer value proposition which is your idea of how you will provide value to your customer. A value proposition is an educated guess that what you are offering will be valuable to the customer. In fact, the entire business model is like a theory about how your company can meet customer needs, and get paid for doing so.[6] You don't know if it will work until you try it. It is also true that the best models are like narratives[7]—you need to be able to explain how all the parts are going to come together to produce this thing that the customer will love. And you also need to explain how you will get revenues by doing so. Will the customer pay for it? Will you sell advertisements? Will you use subscriptions?

The fundamental purpose of business models is to create value for both your customer and your firm.[8] You have to give your customers what they want, even if they're not quite sure what it is. And you have to do it in such a way that they will choose your firm instead of your competitor's. When that happens, an exchange agreement, or a relationship, is formed between you and your customers. You need the revenues that they provide and they need the product or service that you offer. Your job from this point forward is to nurture the relationship and adapt as needed in order to keep it strong. This is complicated because the customers can leave at any time. You can't control them so you have to make them happy.

Eventually, assuming the business gets off the ground, the model will become built into your company. It can be found in the way that you manufacture your products, the type of employees you hire, the brand that you choose, and the policies that you set. Often, this side of the business model is hidden or unclear to organizational participants. People come and go. Time change. Eventually, no one remembers why certain things are done the way they are. The reasons for many past decisions are passed off as tradition. To revitalize your company and your relationship with your customers, you should take a hard look at everything you do and ask yourself how it contributes to building or capturing value. Chances are that you will find some things that no longer make sense. Perhaps they used to be valuable, but now they're not. Learning to make your business model explicit is a big deal. It is often the first step to improvement or change.

Three Business Model Lenses

In my mind, a business model is like a lens—its purpose is to help you see things more clearly.

If you refocus the lens, you can see something different. On the basis of this simple idea, I describe a business model concept that has three lenses based on three levels of complexity. Each level builds on the one beneath it and adds to what you see when you apply the model. The three levels are:

1. Foundation level business model
2. Differentiated business model
3. Adaptive business model

Foundation Business Model

As I said earlier, the most basic purpose of a business model is to create, deliver, and capture value. So the foundation of any business model is putting into place the processes and activities needed to provide an offering to a customer and earn a profit. These basic business model activities are necessary for establishing operations but insufficient to assure competitive advantage. They are often transparent and easy to copy, and as a result, they are often shared by multiple competitors.[9] The foundation level is a fairly generic model regarding what the business is and is not, and ensuring that the pieces fit together to serve the customer.[10] As such, it permits general comparisons across ventures and also is easy to imitate. The foundation business model does not focus on the competition.

Differentiated Business Model

Once you have established a basic system for providing and capturing value, the next step is to ensure that you can attract customers to your offering versus those of competitors. This means that you have to think strategically about your business model and your customer value proposition and build in some ways of ensuring its uniqueness.[11] In other words, you will need to figure out how to build a competitive advantage into your model. This requires providing value that customers perceive as novel, or better, or cheaper than that offered by the competition.[12] And it requires building in means of protecting those novelties from easy imitation.

Adaptive Business Model

Once you gain a customer base, your business model should become more complex. The adaptive business model lens incorporates your customers and your relationship with customers into the model. Incorporating your customers into your thinking about your business model will help you to maintain its viability over time.[13] Adaptation requires listening to customers and reconsidering what it means to provide them with superior value. It requires learning from your customers. In addition, by using this model, you can see ways to use your customer base as a resource. By recognizing and utilizing this resource appropriately, you can sustain and even renew your model over time.

Business Models Versus Strategy

In comparing the idea of a business model with the idea of a strategy, the big difference is that a strategy is a broader concept. But business models come first. To put it simply, a business model is a necessary but not sufficient ingredient of your strategy. Putting together a viable business model will get you in the game. However, once competition comes along, you probably won't get far unless you have a strategy about how to serve your customers better than your competitors.

Strategy describes how a firm competes or differentiates itself from others.[14] According to Michael Porter, strategy involves carrying out different activities than your competitors, or accomplishing similar things in different ways. The bottom line is that strategy is always considered relative to your competitors.[15] Competitive advantage means that you are doing something better, either to create more value for your customers or to capture more value for the firm.

When you create a basic business model, you are developing logic for bringing resources and processes together to generate value for your customers while making money. Strategy is not necessarily involved at this point. And yet, you can only survive without a strategy if there are no competitors in the picture. If you do have competitors, then you must build some differentiators into your model. To this end, you will have to think strategically about how to provide value to your customers that is better, or newer, or cheaper than that provided by others. Your business model then begins to reflect your strategy. And yet, it also limits the kinds of strategic decisions that you can make.

As a simple example, consider the grocery store business. At the foundation level, grocery store business models are based on bringing together an array of foods and household goods in a physical location where customers can come, choose what they want, and pay. The basic value proposition is to provide customers with access to affordable food and beverages and other articles for your home. Essentially, you are giving your customers convenient access to desired items at a good price. Profit margins, in this industry, have traditionally been quite thin.

When you consider ways to differentiate grocery stores, you have many choices. You can provide a broader variety of foods in a more pleasant setting, or a narrower variety of foods at a lower price. You can enhance the services provided or you can have customers do more of the work themselves. There are many ways to build differentiators into the model.

For example, consider how the German firm, Aldi, competes against more traditional supermarkets. Aldi's relatively small stores carry a narrow range of core, high volume grocery items, usually in one size and one brand.[16] You may find different choices on different visits. Products are stacked in boxes, on pallets. There are no meat counters or fresh produce. Prices are rock bottom low but costs are low enough to offset this pricing scheme. All of the pieces of the model are self-reinforcing.[17]

Obviously, Aldi is still using a basic grocery store business model. Customers drive to the store, load up their carts with food and sundries, pay, and depart. But now that model has been tweaked to generate more profit and draw in a particular set of customers. Strategic choices have been built into the business model to generate a slightly different value proposition, and sophisticated processes have been designed to slow down imitation and enhance efficiency.

Business models are not strategies. Business models are the foundations for strategy.[18] They are also the reflections of a firm's realized strategies.[19] Entrepreneurs and managers should think strategically about their business model and build in features and processes that set them apart from competitors. Yet these strategic choices are constrained by the basic business model you started with. And the focus must always be on creating value.

So the bottom line is this. *A business model is a tool or a concept that will help you to build or analyze your company. Your business model is also reflected in the systems and processes that you put into place to create and deliver value to your customers and to capture value for your firm. It is the foundation on which you will build your strategy.* A strategy is a plan or position that distinguishes your firm from competitors who may very well have the same business model.

You can use the business model lenses described in this chapter to help you assess the elements of your business model and to seek ways to build in differentiators that will provide your customers with better value than they can get from others. Moreover, when you think strategically about your business model, you may find ways to build systems and processes that are hard for others to replicate and that may increase your bottom line.[20]

Strategic thinking about your business model is an ongoing requirement. The issues faced in building a brand new model are very different from those that you must think about when your model has matured and new competitors are at your door. To be successful, you must constantly be learning, adapting, and evaluating your decisions and activities.

Value Exchange Relationship

The objective of your business modeling efforts is to create a sustainable exchange of value with your customers. This occurs when both parties are getting something of value. It's a balance between the value provided and the value received. Once you get this relationship going, you have to take care of it. As any married person will tell you, it's one thing to start up the fire, but it's another thing altogether to keep it going. You have to be mindful of the flame itself, as well as everything that is going on around it.

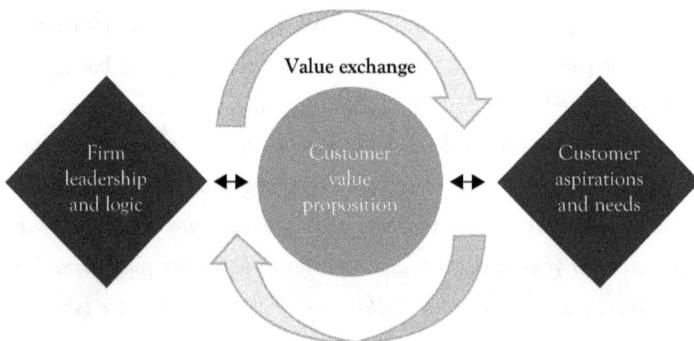

Figure 1.1. Value exchange relationship.

The following questions will help you think about this value exchange relationship.

1. **What do you mean by value?** Business models exist to create and deliver value, both to a customer and to the firm. Therefore, you should begin your thinking about business models by thinking about value. What type of offering will you be bringing to the market and what are its features? How will it be accessed? How will it help someone to achieve a goal or solve a problem?

2. **For whom will you create value?** Who are the customers that will need or want your offering? Where are they located? How will you find them and reach them? What needs or aspirations or problems do they have and what features do they prefer?

3. **How will you create value for the customer and make money doing it?** What is your value proposition and what system will you put in place to make this happen? How will you build your deliverables and brand your products? And how will you manage your costs in order to meet the profit criteria you've established?

4. **How can you provide better value than the competition?** What factors will distinguish your offering from those of other firms? How is your offering different, or better, or cheaper to buy? What are your sources of advantage and how can you protect them from theft or imitation?

5. **How can you strengthen your customer relationships?** Once people start buying your offering, what will you do to keep them coming back? How can you enhance the link that ties you together? Can you put processes in place to enhance the social or emotional components of your connection?

6. **Can you change?** Can you adapt to customers' changing perceptions of value as new technologies and new business models change the game? Can you evolve completely or begin again? It is likely that even successful business models will need to be revamped or abandoned at some point.[21] Can you remodel? Remodeling refers to a complete transformation of a model and reformulation of a new design. It may require you to change your perspective and consider radically new concepts. It may even be best at times to sell the business and begin again.

Testing Your Hypothesis—Four Evolving Concerns

As I mentioned earlier, every entrepreneur or new business starts out with a hypothesis about the customers and the market, and then develops a business model in alignment with that hypothesis.[22] Most likely, your initial model won't be fully formed and you will have to refine it repeatedly as you try it out.[23] First, you need to determine whether you can make it work at all, and then you have to figure out whether you could make money with it. Ultimately, you will never know if your business model is going to work until you've tested it with real customers paying real money. Johnson, Christensen, and Kagermann state that successful new businesses typically revise their business models four times or so on the road to profitability.[24]

Feasibility and *viability* are the two basic concerns that you must address when you stand up your initial model. Will it work? Can you meet your promises to customers? Will they find your offering to be valuable? Will they be willing to pay some money to get it? These questions must be asked by all new entrepreneurs. And they are often addressed in an iterative fashion with small steps and experiments and occasional injections of cash.[25] They sometimes require luck and intuition as you try to figure out what will work. And they always require advice and assistance from as many of your friends and acquaintances as you can draw in.

Sustainability relates to the longer term. Once you are selling something and generating steady revenues, you must shift your focus toward bolstering your relationship with your customers, and differentiating your firm from new entrants. Key questions involve how you can provide value that is superior to the competition and how you can ensure that customers remain interested over time.

Adaptability is a continuing concern. Over time, you will have to revise or evolve your model; worse yet, you may even have to rethink your initial assumptions and make radical changes in the way you do business. You might also choose to harvest your resources and invest them in new ventures and spin offs. Adaptability involves knowing the limits of your current design and sometimes making the hard decision to start all over again.

Summary and Conclusions

In this chapter, I introduced the business model concept, distinguished it from strategy, and introduced three different business model lenses that can help you focus on specific elements of your value creation and capture system. I argued that the development of a business model should be based on strategic thinking, and that you can build differentiators into your model to set it apart from others. I also argued that the business model by itself is not strategy. It is both the foundation for your strategy and a reflection of your strategy-making processes. Finally, I introduced four business model tests that must be passed if your model is to generate value for you and your customers.

These are complex ideas, but I will continue to revisit them throughout this book by sharing stories about how some business models were built, why they work, and sometimes, why they fail. I'm also going to look at the strategies used by people to build their business models, as well as the actions they have taken to sustain them over time, or to change them completely.

In order to frame these stories and clarify the core logics connecting the business models, I will use each of the three business model lenses: the foundation business model, the differentiated business model, and the adaptive business model, as appropriate.

In the next chapter, I will introduce each of the business model lenses in graphic form and I will explain their major components.

CHAPTER 2

Three Business Model Lenses

Until recently, people didn't use the term business model at all—they were built into the way we did things, but they were not openly discussed. Several things came together to change this situation. First, was the growth of business outsourcing, which started in the 1970s and 1980s.[1] Until that time, most large companies controlled their entire value chains from raw materials to distributors, and they were diversified across products and markets. When global competition began heating up, these large enterprises were fat and slow.[2] They had to find a way to simplify their operations.

Some companies slimmed down by outsourcing certain functions that weren't part of the core. For instance, L. L. Bean has outsourced the printing of its catalogs for many years. Next came the outsourcing of administrative support services. Eastman Kodak raised eyebrows when it announced the outsourcing of its information technology systems in 1989, but, these days, a new crop of business service providers, including Accenture, makes a lot of money by providing processes from accounting and billing to employee selection and hiring. Today, some companies even outsource their core functions, including manufacturing. There are plenty of companies out there waiting to do that for you. These new ideas about different ways of organizing have also led to new thinking about business modeling.

The availability of spreadsheets for analyzing your numbers has also contributed to our new fascination with business modeling.[3] Now, when you are trying to figure out what parts of the process to do yourself and what parts to do with partners, you can do what-if analyses. This is important when you are working out your profit formula—a crucial part of any business model.

Finally, both the growth of the Internet, and the movement of business online have led to the emergence and study of new e-business models.[4] These new models have undermined many traditional industries by providing a new level of customer value.[5] For example, Amazon.com changed the way people shop and challenged many traditional retailers by allowing customers to purchase goods from home. Today, Amazon is still blazing a trail with ongoing innovations in its business model, ranging from the Kindle and the amazing growth of online publishing to the addition of online marketplaces, which lower the barriers to entry for new companies seeking a way to get their products in front of their customers. Similarly, Blockbuster's recent demise came about after Netflix fundamentally changed our perception of how to watch movies at home, first through delivery to your mailbox, after ordering online, and then by providing us with video streaming on demand. Owing to innovations like these, traditional business models are under attack, and new ones are constantly being contemplated and implemented.

Yet, the resounding failure of some of these new e-business models has added even more fuel to the fire. How can companies exist with no revenues? How can we charge for online information and services that customers expect to be free? New pricing mechanisms have become major topics of discussion and experimentation. Even today, we don't pay directly to use Google's powerful search engine but the company could not survive if it hadn't been able to figure out how to generate revenue flows.

Thus, with the movement of firms to the Internet, companies have begun to think much more explicitly about the value created and captured by their business models. Even firms that do only part of their business online have had to rethink their distribution decisions, if not their entire business models.[6] And with the increasing interconnectedness of markets, some companies can move, and grow, extremely fast. Consider Groupon, which came into existence in 2008 and went public in 2011, with a market value over $17 billion.[7]

Today, business models are frequent topics of conversation and concern. In the next sections, I define what a business model is and describe its elements.

Business Model Definition and Elements

Cantrell and Linder have said that what many people call a business model is really only part of a business model.[8] I agree. Consider how one recent online post described three types of business models: bricks and clicks, bait and hook, and subscription.[9] This is overly simplistic. The key to remember is that a business model is not just a pricing mechanism, or a logistics chain, or a slogan; instead, it is the entire system of resources and processes that you will put in place to create and capture value.

Today, some excellent blogs and columns are being written online about business model development and innovation. Some of the leaders are Clay Christensen, Marc Johnson, Alex Osterwilder, and Steve Blank. I have included references to their work at the end of this book. A growing number of academic articles also are being published on this topic, including important articles by Magretta, Teece, Schweizer, Chesbrough, and many others. In their comprehensive review of the business model literature published in 2011, Zott, Amit, and Massa concluded the following:

1. The business model is emerging as a new level of analysis. It is different from strategy.
2. Business models take a system-level holistic approach to explaining how firms do business.
3. Firm activities play an important role in how business models are carried out.
4. Business models explain how value is crafted, not just captured.[10]

In other words, we create business models to explain how firm resources and activities come together as a system to create and capture value. To design a business model, we have to decide what we mean by value (for both our customers and ourselves), and we have to figure out how to bring together the elements needed to make it happen in such a way that it will not easily be duplicated or outperformed.

One perspective that has been particularly useful in my own understanding of what belongs in a business model is from Johnson, Christensen, and Kagerman.[11] Johnson wrote more about this model in his book *Seizing the White Space*.[12] According to these authors, a business model consists of the following four interlocking elements that, taken together, create and deliver value:

- **Key resources** are things that you will use to build your business model and the way in which you will get them.
- **Key processes** are the routines and capabilities you will use to turn your resources into something of value for your customers.
- **The profit formula** is how you evaluate whether you can make money on the things you are doing to deliver value to your customer.
- **The customer value proposition** explains clearly what benefits you intend to provide to your customer through your product or service offering.[13] It is the most important of the four elements.

Taken together, these four components provide the initial ingredients for business modeling, but I contend that you can refine your ideas by adding three additional pieces to the mix.

- **The entrepreneur or firm leaders' goals, aspirations, and capabilities.** Every entrepreneur or leader comes to the business with personal aspirations and values as well as particular ambitions related to time, scope, and size of the enterprise.[14] In addition, each company leader has highly specific experience and education, which shape his methods of bringing together a business model. If we provide two packages of identical resources to two different people, they are likely to come up with very different models based on their personal capabilities and goals. This explains why venture capitalists are always much interested in the founder's experience and drive when they consider whether to fund a start-up. It is this person, or team, that makes everything happen, at least at the beginning. As a result, you should begin your business modeling by doing some deep reflection on your own goals and capabilities.

- **The customers.** Most business model formulations talk about the importance of the customer as the receiver of value and provider of revenues, but they do not include the customer in the model.[15] Osterwilder includes the customer as one of the nine components of his business model canvas but only as the target of the value proposition and generator of revenues. Customers are not involved as part of the infrastructure or in the definition of the offer.[16] However, Chesbrough[17] talks about open business models in which various partners, including customers, participate in the innovation process. In addition, some marketing researchers have begun looking at coproduction in which the customer participates in the creation of the core offering itself.[18]
- **The relationship between the firm and its customers.** Once the firm has established the exchange of value with customers, a relationship is formed. This relationship must be nurtured and cared for if it is to be sustained.

The next section shows how these components can be brought together to form three different business model lenses including the foundation business model, the differentiated model, and the adaptive business model.

Three Business Model Lenses

Figure 2.1 shows the business model foundation, which includes the four elements described by Johnson, Christensen, and Kagerman and the firm entrepreneur or leadership team in the middle.

In the first stage of business modeling, the goal is to figure out how to combine resources and develop processes to generate a value proposition that will benefit your customers while also generating a profit for you. This lens focuses only on the elements of the business that you have to work to create and capture value.

1. What capabilities do we need to
   make or sell our offer?
2. Should we do these ourselves, or
   outsource them?

1. What resources do we
   need to make or sell
   our offer?
2. Do we control these,
   or do we get them
   from partners?

1. What features will we
   offer our customers?
2. At what price?
3. How will they access it?
4. How will they experience
   the product and the
   purchase interaction?

Key
processes

Key
resources

Firm
aspirations
& goals

Value
proposition

Profit
formula

1. What margins do we need?
2. What are our overhead costs?
3. What is the breakeven volume?

1. What is our vision for this
   business?
2. For ourselves?
3. What skills do we bring
   to the table?

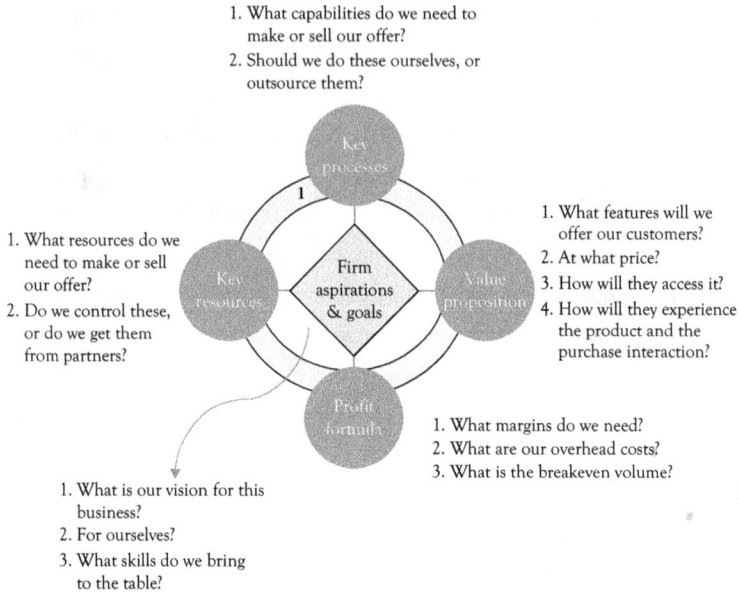

Figure 2.1. Foundation business model lens.

The *customer value proposition* is the most important part of your business model foundation. You can think of the value proposition as a hypothesis on how you will provide and deliver value to customers. In fact, at the beginning, your whole business model is like a theory of how all the pieces will come together to create and capture value.

Creating an attractive value proposition is tricky because sometimes your perception of benefits provided and the customers' perception of benefits received may be very different. Only the customer can decide if something is really a benefit.[19] And many would-be entrepreneurs have missed the mark. I recently read about a man who opened up a day care center for cats. As a cat owner, I can't imagine how anyone could have believed that would work. The point is that your initial business model reflects your hypothesis about what customers want, and you will never know whether it is going to work until you test it. Of course, the better you know your customer, the better your proposition is likely to be.

You need access to *key resources* and the ability to carry out *key processes* in order to bring your value proposition to life. In fact, your whole idea may have come about because of access to a key resource or experience you've had with a particular process. For instance, you may have a patent on a new product design or you may have inherited some money. A generic list of resources includes things such as people, technologies, products, equipment, channels, and established brands; however, almost anything can be a resource if you have an open mind or a good imagination. Your family name can be a resource if it is well known, and your relationships with friends or even your social networks can be resources as well.

Key processes are things that you know how to do, or to get done. These include all the processes you will use to make things and sell things. How will you manufacture? How will you advertise? How will you deliver the products? How will you develop and motivate your employees?

As you consider the resources and processes needed to create your value proposition, a key question to ask time and again is: What activities should be carried out inside or outside the company? What can you do by yourself and what should be outsourced? This is a fundamental decision in business modeling.

At this point in modeling your business, you also have to take a good hard look at yourself and your leadership team. What skills do you bring to the table? What limitations do you have? Have you considered these strengths and weaknesses in conjunction with your assessment of key resources and processes? In addition, what are your long-term goals? Are you in this business for the long run or are you trying to build and sell quickly? And, of course, what is your vision for the firm itself? Are you striving to create a local institution, or to achieve global dominance? The better you understand these driving forces, the stronger your leadership will be. In addition, knowing what you are trying to achieve in the long run will help you clarify your thinking about your economic objectives.

The *profit formula* portion of the foundation model requires you to think specifically about how you are going to make money for your company. To answer this question, you need to consider your sources of revenue, whether from sales, advertising, subscriptions, or some combination. Once you know where the revenues are coming from, you must consider three essential elements: your margin, your overhead, and your required breakeven volume.

The margin is the price you charge for a product or service minus the direct costs of producing it. Direct costs include the cost of labor and materials used to make the product or carry out the service. Next is overhead, which are the costs you incur regardless of whether you sell anything or not. These include rent, electricity, administrative support, and so on. David Newton refers to this as the burn, or the money that will be spent regardless of the level of production.[20] Finally, breakeven volume is the number of products a firm must sell at a given margin (price–direct costs) to cover the overhead costs of the firm. If you fail to meet this breakeven volume, then your firm will incur a loss for a given period.

At the end of this stage of modeling, you should have an idea that is ready to be tested. You will know that it works if customers are willing to pay money to get your offering, and if you find that you could maintain your operations based on that revenue flow.

Note that the business model foundation includes the customer value proposition, but it does not really include your relationship with your customer. Again, this is because the business model foundation is a hypothesis. Once this design is laid out, it must be tested to see if it attracts customers. You will need to promote, experiment, and revise your approach until you have enough evidence to support the idea that people will really be willing to buy your product at a price that will cover your costs and produce a profit.

One other thing that is missing in your business model foundation is a way to differentiate your offer from competitors. Differentiation is not built into this foundational model and so it is fairly easy to replicate.[21] Figure 2.2 shows a model to be used in the second stage of business modeling—the differentiated business model.

While the foundation model captures the essence of the business model for many firms, sustainable competitive advantage depends on the addition of unique approaches and difficult-to-imitate processes to one or more of the foundational components.[22] Thus, loop 2 represents the addition of differentiators to the foundation that will provide the customer with something that is better or cheaper, or just plain newer, than competitive offerings. In addition, this level of the model requires you to think about how to provide value in such a way that it cannot be easily copied.

1. Do we have access to processes
   that others cannot imitate?
2. Can we combine processes and
   resources in ways that others cannot?

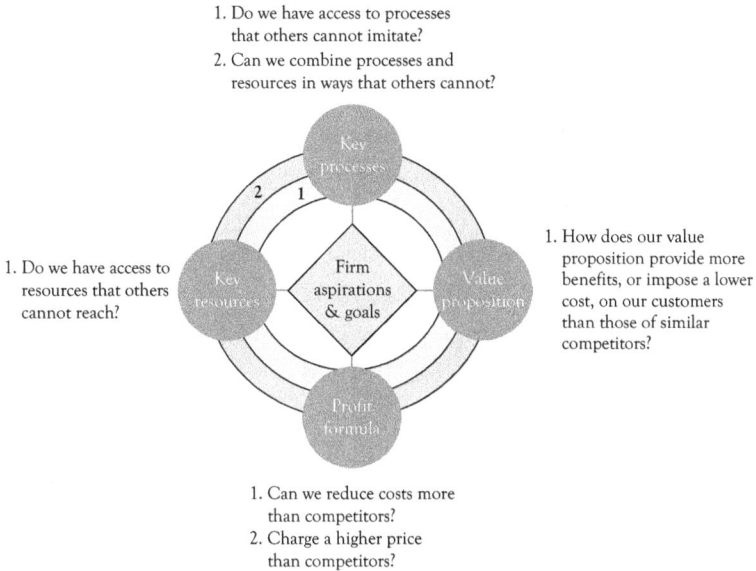

1. Do we have access to
   resources that others
   cannot reach?

1. How does our value
   proposition provide more
   benefits, or impose a lower
   cost, on our customers
   than those of similar
   competitors?

1. Can we reduce costs more
   than competitors?
2. Charge a higher price
   than competitors?

Figure 2.2. Differentiated business model lens.

Examples of questions to be added to your business modeling at this point include the following:

- How does our value proposition provide more benefits, or impose fewer costs, on our customers than those of similar competitors?
- Do we have access to resources that others cannot reach?
- Do we have access to processes that others cannot imitate?
- Can we combine our processes and resources in ways that others cannot?
- Can we reduce costs more than competitors?
- Can we charge higher prices than our competitors?

Separating the business model foundation from the differentiated business model is actually an oversimplification. Obviously, some business models are built in a unique way from the very beginning. In fact, if you are planning to enter a market in which competition already exists, then you must build differentiators into your model from the very beginning, or it doesn't even make sense to do it. However, in other cases, it makes sense to experiment with your basic model operating system before messing with differentiators, just to ensure that you've got something that works.

If your business model is different enough, you may find that your approach may come to change the way business is done in a particular industry, as Apple did when it turned mobile phones into portable computers. Or you may establish a completely new niche by adding value where there was none. This is what Kim and Mauborgne called a Blue Ocean strategy.[23] It means opening up a whole new market and escaping the bloody red market that is saturated with competitors. This is what Nintendo did by designing its Wii gaming console for people who were not current video game users.

Thus, there will always be cases in which loops one and two are compressed. I have separated them here only to make it clear that one should think about creating and capturing value (loop 1) and think about doing these things differently from competitors (loop 2). Both considerations are highly important.

Your initial goal in building a business model is to make something that your customers want to buy. Once this happens, you can start earning money. But your thinking can't stop there. You also need to give them a reason to buy from you rather than anyone else.

Once the system is established, and once customers begin paying for the offer, the third stage of business modeling begins. At this point, you can use another business model lens to stimulate your thinking. This lens adds two new elements to your business model—your customer base and your relationship with your customer. The adaptive business model lens is shown in Figure 2.3. It includes the foundation and differentiators as well as the exchange relationship connecting the customer to the firm.

The model in Figure 2.3 is called an adaptive business model because it focuses your attention on your customers and your ongoing relationship with them. The value exchange relationship is like the engine that propels your business model forward. It is initiated by providing deliverables that your customers appreciate and are willing to purchase, and it is fueled by your firm's ability to capture those payments and reinvest them in the system.[24] Without attention and consideration, this newly hatched relationship can expire.

Your relationship with customers is actually a social agreement indicating that both parties want to do business together. You agree to

1. How can we facilitate customer
   to customer communication
   and learning?
2. How can we learn from our
   customers?

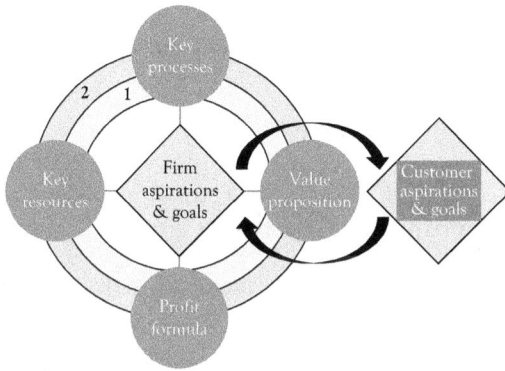

1. How satisfied are our
   customers with our
   offering?
2. How satisfied are
   customers with our
   relationship?
3. What long term goals and
   concerns are driving our
   customers? Can we
   assist?
4. What current concerns or
   costs do our customers
   still face even when using
   our product?
5. What new alternatives or
   substitutes are selected by
   customers when they
   leave us?

Figure 2.3. Adaptive business model lens.

provide the value that they seek, and they agree to purchase. Revenues generated by this exchange agreement are crucial to the business—but customers are fickle and their perception of value may shift in the blink of an eye. To maintain this relationship, you must adopt specific actions and processes to help you to stay in sync with emerging customer attitudes and behaviors. Throughout this book, I give examples of companies that have done this very well, and companies that have done it poorly or not at all.

Companies that consider their customers and customer relationships as part of their business model can gain advantages that others miss. These days, it is well known that customers not only generate value in the form of revenues, but they can also help coproduce products and services, assist in promoting and selling your offer to others, and stimulate new ideas for ongoing innovations.

Questions to be addressed in this model include:

- How satisfied are our customers with our offering?
- How satisfied are our customers with our relationship?
- What long-term goals and concerns are driving our customers?
  Can we assist?

- What current concerns or costs do our customers still face even when using our product?
- What new alternatives or substitutes are selected by customers when they leave us?
- How can we facilitate customer-to-customer communication and learning?
- How can we learn from our customers?

Modeling Your Business

The foundation business model lens can be useful when you are first developing your business model, and you simply want to focus on how you will create value for a customer and capture value for your firm. It can assist you in generating your theory or hypothesis about how your offering will provide customer value.[25] It also includes a profit formula component to stimulate you to think specifically about the revenues you will need to gain, as well as how to keep your costs in line so that you can make a profit. Overall, the key is to build a concise, logical description of how the different parts of the business will come together to create value for the customer and make money for the firm.

Once you have figured out how the parts should work together to generate value, you will need to test your ideas for feasibility and viability. That is, does it work as planned? Will people buy it? While you are building the foundation of your business model, you should be constantly experimenting and testing to see what works. You've got a theory about how to generate and capture value and you need to test it to see if it will do what it is supposed to do, and if it will attract paying customers.

If this pans out, you also need to be sure that you can differentiate your offer from those of competitors and take steps to avoid imitation. The differentiated model is based on the premise that you must provide customers with *superior* value—so that they will choose to buy from you versus another supplier. You will need to build differentiators into your model to gain an advantage over your competition.

Finally, you need to consider ways to nurture and sustain the value exchange cycle that you have created with your customer base. Specific processes and policies will be needed as you grow. The adaptive business model lens brings your customer into your business modeling processes once a relationship has been established. Your customers can be considered a resource that you can draw upon as you adapt your model over time. In addition, you will need to consider ways to nourish and sustain customer relationships. This may eventually lead to reconsideration of initial modeling decisions. Taken as a whole, the adaptive business model lens is a tool that can help you sustain and renew your business.

As an entrepreneur, you can use these lenses to begin modeling your business idea. If you work for a business, you can use them to clarify the core logic behind your company's value proposition. You should be able to tell how you will make things, how you sell things, and how these activities can generate value for your customers and your firm.[26] Just think of it as a story. If you can't tell it simply, as a narrative, it's probably broken.[27]

Summary and Conclusions

In this chapter, I described changes in the business environment that have contributed to the growth in thinking about business models; I introduced seven key components of business models; and I used these components to create three business model lenses. These included the foundation business model lens, the differentiated business model lens, and the adaptive business model lens.

Each of these lenses is based on the premise that, to be effective, a business model must be built in a way to create, deliver, and capture value. Before delving further into the modeling process, we need to take a closer look at what we mean by value. Chapter 3 suggests that value is best understood from the perspective of the customer.

CHAPTER 3

How the Bomgar Box Delivers Customer Value

Every business model is built to attract paying customers. It does this by creating and delivering something that they value. And value, it turns out, cannot be objectively defined or determined except through the eyes of the customer.[1] The idea that value is subjective is an important one. It literally means that your product or service will have no value unless some customers somewhere believe that it does.

Customers view products or services to be valuable if they help them to accomplish a goal, solve a problem, increase a benefit, or reduce a cost. Something is even more valuable if it helps them to accomplish several of these at once, such as cleaning the kitchen without harming the environment; or dressing fashionably while saving money. Thus, to generate an attractive value proposition, you have to figure out who are the customers, what do they want to accomplish, and what are the sacrifices that are currently associated with getting it done.

Joel Bomgar didn't have any of these problems. His highly successful product, the Bomgar Box, was driven by a keen understanding of a very specific customer's unmet needs. Why did he understand them so well? Because he was the customer!

A Frustrated Computer Technician and College Student

In 2002, Joel was a senior at Bellhaven College in Jackson, Mississippi, working his way through school as a part-time IT support representative. Given his need to balance work and school demands, he was frustrated by the fact that he often spent twice as much time driving to meet clients as he did fixing their computer problems.[2] As a result, he began working on a system that would enable him to view and correct problems remotely from his own desktop. "I hacked together a piece of technology I didn't really intend to sell," he said. "It was really just to make my work easier. But I figured I couldn't be the only tech support person on the planet that had these frustrations."[3]

Shortly after graduation, he began promoting the software through an html page he wrote for the purpose. In his first two months of business, Bomgar sold 50 licenses at $500 dollars apiece,[4] a sure sign of viability for his fledgling business.

Less than a decade later, Bomgar's appliance-based products help organizations improve tech support efficiency and performance by enabling them to securely support nearly any device or system, anywhere in the world—including Windows, Mac, Linux, iOS, Android, and more. More than 6,500 organizations across 65 countries have deployed Bomgar to improve customer satisfaction while dramatically reducing costs. The company reported $31 million in revenue in 2011, and had approximately 200 employees working in 6 offices, including hubs in London and Paris.[5] At 32, Bomgar remains its CEO.

A good example of a satisfied Bomgar customer is Boston-based Houghton Mifflin Harcourt Publishing (HMHP) Company, the world's largest publisher of educational materials for prekindergarten to high schools. In addition to its traditional textbooks and testing materials, the company sells educational software, including math and reading software for students, as well as server software that allows school districts to build portal sites. Overall, the publisher's tech-support staff receives 100,000 calls a year, with over 40,000 of them ringing in from August through mid-October, at the start of each new school year.[6] Trying to deal with this spike in demand each fall was an ongoing issue. In addition, 20% of its calls were from Macintosh users and the product they were formerly using only supported PCs.[7]

HMHP switched over to Bomgar in 2007 because it offered more features and was less expensive.[8] In addition to supporting Mac users, the Bomgar Box also allowed HMHP's employees to exchange instant messages with customers, which was important because many teachers don't have phones in their classrooms or computer labs. Additionally, the Bomgar system allows two technicians to log into the same session, which is helpful if one support representative needs a colleague to help resolve a call. This feature also allows new tech-support trainees to log into a session and watch experienced staffers troubleshoot.[9] According to the HMHP personnel, once the tech-support center implemented the Bomgar remote-support tool, it saw an immediate return on investment, including faster call resolution, more calls handled per worker, and lower costs.

Bomgar's remote-administration tool has made the job faster and easier for HMHP's tech-support team who admit that they "couldn't live without it."[10] In the next section, I explore three ways that the Bomgar box provides value to its customers: (a) By helping them achieve long-term goals; (b) by solving a pressing problem; and (c) by adding benefits and reducing costs.

A Hierarchy of Customer Value

Three decades of marketing research strongly suggests that perceived value is based on assessing product costs and benefits in relation to goals and objectives.[11] We can see how this works using Woodruff's[12] customer value hierarchy, depicting three levels of customer goals and purposes (Figure 3.1).

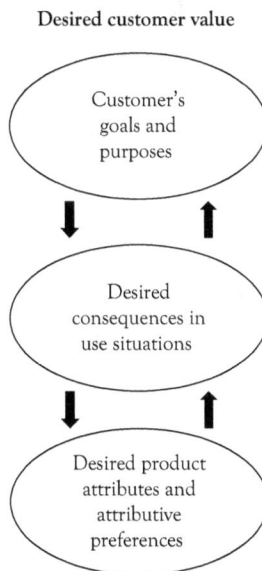

Desired customer value

Customer's goals and purposes

Desired consequences in use situations

Desired product attributes and attributive preferences

Figure 3.1. The customer value hierarchy.

According to Woodruff, customers think about value in a means–end way.[13] If we start at the top of the hierarchy, we can see that the customers' long-term goals and purposes shape the desired consequences in use or current job to be done. In turn, the thing that the customer is trying to get done right now shapes his or her preferences for particular kinds of product features.

If we start at the bottom of the hierarchy, we begin by observing that customers think about products as bundles of specific attributes. These attributes are evaluated on the basis of their ability to facilitate the achievement of desired consequences, or jobs, at the middle level of the hierarchy. These consequences are important because they allow customers to move toward their long-term aspirations and purposes.

Applying these three levels of customer goals to the HMHP company helps explain the high value the firm places on the Bomgar Box. The company's long-term goals include growth and return on investment, and its fundamental purpose is to help students learn. These economic and social goals affect its desired consequences in use, or the problems that computer technicians run into when trying to assist teachers from afar. With customers all around the world, the tech-support team can do this much more quickly and easily by using the Bomgar box to access the teachers' computers. At the lowest level, some particular attributes of interest include the product's ability to connect with many types of computer hardware, its instant messaging capability, and the ability to sign on multiple technicians at one time.

So, to understand whether a customer will perceive value in a particular product or service, you must consider three things: (a) What are the customer's long-term goals and purposes? (b) What is the job that the customer is trying to get done right now in light of these goals? (c) How does the customer evaluate the costs and benefits of particular product attributes in getting this job done? Let's look at each of these drivers in more detail.

Helping Customers Achieve Long-Term Goals and Purposes

Huffman Ratneshwar, and Mick[14] describe the highest level of customer goals and purposes as life themes, or personal ideals of living, including chosen life roles and identities. As we go through life, all of us develop deeply held beliefs about certain ideals or certain end states of existence[15] such as freedom, education, or family unity. Similarly, we come to identify ourselves within certain roles or identities, such as teacher, father, or successful manager. These deeply held beliefs are reflected in our long-term goals and commitments, both for ourselves and for our families or communities. Research has shown that life themes are limited in number within an individual, and that, once established, they rarely change.[16] Together with life roles, they represent core conceptions of self,[17] and are easily activated across a variety of circumstances.[18] Moreover, once internalized, these aspirations serve as standards to guide many shorter-term decisions and actions.[19]

As customers, our identities along with our long-term goals and values may affect our preferences for particular kinds of products or services, or the way we evaluate the costs and benefits of particular product attributes. We may be more willing to pay extra for certain benefits that appeal to our values, or we may be willing to sacrifice our time or money in order to be part of something that we find meaningful.

Many companies have built successful business models based on their understanding of their customers' aspirations and self-identity. Dapple, for instance, is a company formed by two mothers whose mission is to create natural cleaning products for households with children. The company sells baby-safe products made from nontoxic ingredients found in nature that are also proven to tackle unique baby cleaning challenges.[20] The company was started by moms to appeal to moms. It aims at their desire to be the best moms possible. It does this by also solving specific problems.

Solving a Customer's Problem

Johnson, Christensen, and Hagerman say that every customer value proposition should begin by helping customers to get an important job done.[21] By job, they mean a "fundamental problem in a given situation that needs a solution" (p. 52). They go on to say that once we understand the job and all its dimensions, we can design the offering. In fact, the more important the job to the customer, the customer satisfaction with current options for getting the job done, the more likely it is that you will be able to produce real customer value.[22]

In a popular You-Tube video, Harvard Business School's Clay Christensen talks about "milkshake marketing."[23] In his talk, he tells a story about trying to help a fast food chain figure out what job customers were trying to get done when, in his words, "they hired a milkshake" for breakfast.[24] After observing and interviewing customers, they learned the following:

> "Most of them, it turned out, bought [the milkshake] to do a similar job. They faced a long, boring commute and needed something to keep that extra hand busy and to make the commute more interesting. They weren't yet hungry, but knew that they'd be hungry by 10 a.m.; they wanted to consume something now that would stave off hunger until noon. And they faced constraints: They were in a hurry, they were wearing work clothes, and they had (at most) one free hand." The milkshake was hired in lieu of a bagel or doughnut because it was relatively tidy and appetite-quenching, and because trying to suck a thick liquid through a thin straw gave customers something to do with their boring commute. Understanding the job to be done, the company could then respond by creating a morning milkshake that was even thicker (to last through a long commute) and more interesting (with chunks of fruit) than its predecessor."[25]

As Christensen's milkshake story shows, the word "job" is used very broadly to describe whatever it is that a customer is trying to accomplish at a particular time whether it involves working or dining, or being entertained or trying to take a nap. These needs may relate to hobbies, habits, or professions.

According to Christopher et al.,[26] to provide something of value to a customer, you must always begin by indentifying what he or she is trying to do with your firm's offering at a particular time and place. Woodruff [27] calls this the customer's use situation. Solving a problem for a customer begins by trying to understand what he or she is trying to do, and what is making it difficult.

Joel Bomgar solved a big problem for computer technicians who were hindered in their ability to serve their distant clients. However, when asked directly why HPHM switched over to Bomgar's products, Robert Baird, manager of HMHP's technical support center in Fort Worth, Texas, said it was because Bomgar offered more features and was less expensive than their prior solution. According to Woodruff's hierarchy, the usage situation, or the job to be done, shapes customers' preferences for particular attributes and desired attribute performance. The next section talks about how customers find value in product attributes and features.

Providing Benefits and Reducing Sacrifices

Multiple benefits and costs are considered by customers when determining the use value of an item. In making this valuation, customers at least implicitly compare perceived benefits against other noneconomic costs, or sacrifices, such as the time, effort, psychic or physical energy required to buy or utilize the product or service, and against the actual exchange value required to pay for those benefits.[28] Obviously, the greatest use-value derives from offerings that are believed to yield the most benefits and require the least expenditure of resources.

The use value of any product offering relates to its perceived performance, as well as possible physical, social, or emotional outcomes, which may be positive or negative depending on the customer.[29] Physical outcomes could include the possibility of getting hurt (a sacrifice) versus the possibility of improving your health or physical attractiveness in some way (benefits). Social outcomes could be negative, if I am concerned that the use of the product will make me look silly, or older; they could be positive if they make me feel similar to someone I admire, or if they lead to my involvement in a community. Emotional outcomes could involve anger or frustration if the product is difficult to use or does not meet my expectations. However, by using a product I may feel happier or more confident. Indeed, I may feel that a product fits into my lifestyle and improves my self-efficacy. I will speak more on this level of outcomes soon. The important point in this discussion is that through their use of a product, customers translate its features into benefits and sacrifices. Based on those, they make their determinations about whether or not to buy.

Often these value calculations require trade-offs.[30] For example, a desired benefit may be reduced or sacrificed in return for larger amounts of other benefits. Or some aspect of expended cost (time or effort) may be traded off against price. In a slow economy, for instance, a consumer may be willing to drive further in order to purchase a product for a reduced price. The extent to which trade-offs are made can vary widely with aspects of the current situation or one's self identity or values. On the one hand, a customer may be willing to accept fewer benefits when buying an object for home use than he or she would if it was needed for the office. On the other hand, a mother might expect more benefits from a product she is buying for her baby versus one for herself.

Although I seem to be implying that the customers' processes of weighing various costs and benefits, and even making trade-offs among them, are quite rational and systematic, this is not always the case. Research shows that these calculations are subjective and individual and vary among consumers.[31] Moreover, some evidence suggests that the weighing of costs and benefits does not always take place consciously and consumers may depend on cues to form impressions of value.[32]

Marketing researchers have long known that customers do not consider all potential benefits equally.[33] Some benefits may be more central to their calculations because they relate to deeply held values, life themes, and cultural or social goals. Also, a person might evaluate the same product differently at different times. Price may be the most important consideration at the time of purchase but a good manual may be more important at the time of assembly.[34] Evidence also suggests that more knowledgeable consumers may gain greater value from particular product or service attributes than others.[35] Someone who knows every feature on his or her smartphone will certainly enjoy it more than someone who barely knows how to answer a call.

One way that customers assign value to your product is to evaluate the benefits derived from using it versus the sacrifices. While there is no set list of benefits and sacrifices, they can be physical, emotional, or social and they may relate to the utility of the product or service itself, or to the ease of accessing or maintaining it, the ease of learning how to use it, the enjoyment it provides, or the friends that it helps them to make.

If this seems complex, it is. And yet we do know that product benefits and costs tend to be evaluated in light of a context. That is, product features are more likely to be viewed as benefits if they help the customer to get a job done right now, or if they help to achieve long-term goals, or if they fit with our personal self-image and values. HMHP Company's tech support group loved Bomgar's multiplatform capability, its instant messaging, and its ability to sign on multiple technicians because they could do their jobs better and faster than before. It allowed them to do their jobs better, thereby helping the company to succeed.

What Do You Value?

Although this chapter has focused on explaining how our customers perceive value, I should point out that the same drivers of customer perceived value also relate to you. As an entrepreneur or a manager, you also enter the value exchange relationship in hopes of achieving multiple levels of goals and objectives. Table 3.1 compares the three levels of motivators or drivers for both firms and their customers.

Huffman Ratneshwar, and Mick suggest that the highest level of goals relate to broad life themes and values associated with "Being;" the middle level goals relate to "Doing," and the lowest level relates to "Having."[36] I mention this here because business models must be designed to create value for both the customer and the firm. What each party perceives as valuable is shaped by an array of aspirations and considerations.

Table 3.1. Three Levels of Drivers for Firms and Customers

	Firm or entrepreneur	Customer
Being—What is our place in the world?	Vision and values	Aspirations and Self-identity
Doing—What do we need to get done?	Mission and strategy	Current concerns or job to be done
Having—What do we hope to gain?	Economic and Social Returns	Benefits and Costs

Designing Your Deliverables to Provide Customer Value

When you design your product or service offering for customers, it is based on your best guess about how your customer defines value. Keep in mind that it is not just your product or service itself that contributes to this assessment. Your deliverables include the following: (a) the actual product or service; (b) the price; (c) the customer's ability to access it; and (d) the actual purchase transaction or interaction.

- The product or service is the core of your offering. Obviously it has to do what it says it is going to do. Functionality and quality are two key issues here. Moreover, it has to do it without causing harm to the customer; better yet if it can make some experience more pleasant. Many other factors go into customer evaluations of your product depending, of course, on what it is. Suffice it to say that the actual mix of features that you select will be evaluated and judged.

- The price of your product or service is important. Too high and it will turn customers off, too low and your product may be viewed as cheap. For services or online offerings, the way you price is important. This is called your pricing mechanism. Popular pricing mechanisms for online firms are freemiums, pay walls, and pay-per-use mechanisms. Appendix A lists many such mechanisms that can be considered when developing your model.

- Access refers to whatever your customers have to do to get or use your product. Can they get it at Walmart? Can they get it online? Do they have to drive to the next town? Do they have to wait for an appointment? Do they have to wait until it comes to their town? There are often obstacles that make it difficult for a customer to access your product or service. If you can make it easier, you are reducing a sacrifice. However, sometimes, limited access can be a sort of benefit if it provides some status to those who get it first.

  The Internet has opened the door to many new businesses by providing a simple, inexpensive means of providing customers with access to your products and services. Consider the explosion in sales of self-published books on Amazon today. Check out the many different handmade products available for sale on Etsy. com. Appendix B provides you with a list of online marketplaces that can be very useful in reaching out to your customers.

- *Transactions and interactions.* A transactional encounter is one that is purely focused on the task, say checking out a customer in a convenience store, or delivering a pizza. If the service provider is simply going through the motions to carry out the purchase, then it is a simple transaction. An interaction, by contrast, occurs when the participants are actually communicating, and forming a relationship. Any transaction also has the potential to become an interaction if the service provider cares about making it happen and takes an interest in what the customers have to say. Customers will often return to particular shops or stores because they enjoy the relationship with the clerk or beautician, or advisor. Interactions can be very important contributors to customers' perceptions of value.

Summary and Conclusions

Let's return briefly to the story of Joel Bomgar that opened this chapter. Joel Bomgar was a computer technician trying to work and go to college. He was strapped for money and time and he was tired of wasting so much time driving to his customer's offices to fix relatively simple problems. Joel never intended to start his own business; he simply wanted to find a way to do his own job more effectively. His business model made sense because he completely understood the situational demands faced by many computer technicians and he was able to design a product to solve a frustrating problem and help them to do their jobs better.

In addition, Bomgar knew how to instill his offering with attributes that customers perceived to be valuable. His initial decision to put the software in a box versus on the cloud was an example of a feature that appealed to his users. Its pricing had options for different sizes of business. His website is full of information and forums for discussion and ongoing learning, all of which are beneficial to the professionals who use his products.

The next chapter begins with the story of another business founder who also had an intuitive understanding of his customer. I show how this business leader took this understanding and built it into a highly effective venture using the foundation and differentiated business model lenses described in Chapter 2.

CHAPTER 4

A Ham Radio Company Builds a Superior Business Model

Martin Jue is a soft-spoken man with large passions. Right now, he is passionate about business models. To him, it is obvious what you have to do to make a business work. You have to sell something he says. That's the main thing.

Martin is the founder of MFJ Enterprises, a leader in the ham radio industry. Today, it is estimated that there are over 600,000 ham radio operators in the United States and over 2 million worldwide. Ham radio operators are a close-knit community, attending hamfests, which are both tradeshows and social gatherings, communicating with each other over the air waves, and listening. Martin's ham number is K5FLU. In this eccentric industry, this Asian-looking man with the Mississippi Delta accent is a star.

In fact, Martin's company, MFJ Enterprises, has just celebrated its 40th anniversary. It hosted a huge picnic for the event, with door prizes, factory tours, tailgating, free forums/discussions, and FCC license exams. Hundreds of people attended, from local officials and university students, to visiting industry leaders from the American Radio Relay League, Ham Nation, and other groups from all over the country. One major guest was Chip Margelli, the marketing director at CQ Magazine who once challenged world champion text messengers to a race on the Jay Leno show to see whether cellular text messaging or radio-based Morse code could send messages faster. "By using Morse code, he beat those guys by far," Jue said.[1]

When I asked Martin why MFJ's business model was so successful, he laughed and said it was the best kind of business model—the cheap kind. To me, his description is overly simplistic. Yes, his company is notoriously cheap with regard to its facilities, offices, and so forth. But it also sells more pieces of ham radio equipment than anyone else in the business. That MFJ leads the industry on innovation is directly due to Martin's personal capabilities as an electrical engineer, and his love of ham radio. He built his first radio at 8 years of age. He had a ham radio license at age 16.

I will use Martin's company as an example as I discuss the five elements comprising the foundation and differentiated business model lenses. Although I discuss the elements in a particular order, an order that helps me to tell Martin's story, I want to emphasize that you can think about these components in any order, depending on how they relate to your initial idea, and which ones stimulate your thinking right now. The purpose of using a model like this is to help you bring the different aspects of your thinking together and to create a logic for doing things that makes sense both to you and to your customers.

Thinking Through MFJ's Business Model Foundation

Figure 4.1 depicts MFJ's foundation business model. As you can see, it includes four elements—Key Resources, Key Processes, the Profit

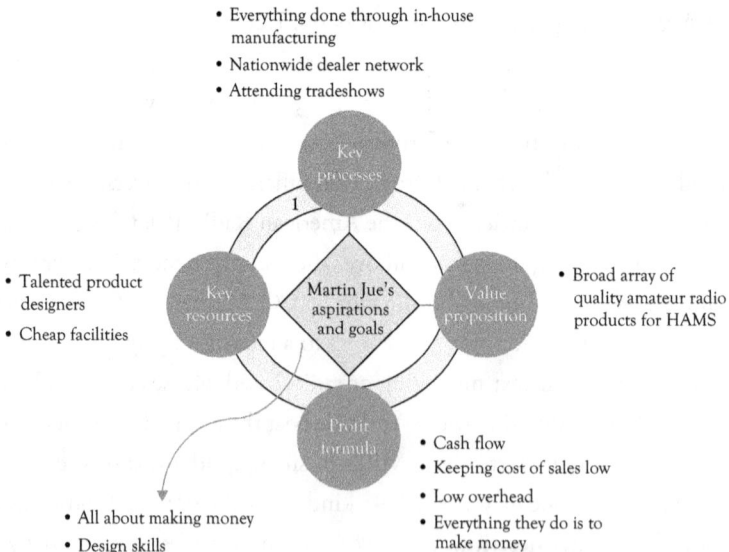

- Everything done through in-house manufacturing
- Nationwide dealer network
- Attending tradeshows

- Talented product designers
- Cheap facilities

Key processes

Key resources

Martin Jue's aspirations and goals

Value proposition

Profit formula

- Broad array of quality amateur radio products for HAMS

- Cash flow
- Keeping cost of sales low
- Low overhead
- Everything they do is to make money

- All about making money
- Design skills

Figure 4.1. MFJ foundation business model.

Formula, and the Customer Value Proposition[2] plus the firm leadership in the center.

Firm aspirations and goals drive all business modeling decisions. For start-ups, these derive from the entrepreneur and the management team based on their vision and values, experience, and capabilities. As a leader, your vision, long-term goals, and values help determine the kind of market you are interested in serving and whether you are seeking high growth or stable income. In an income-driven model, the entrepreneur will invest to the point that the business can generate an ongoing and stable income for the principals. In a growth model, investment and reinvestment are sought in an attempt to grow the value of the firm to the point that it will generate capital gains for investors.[3]

When Martin was young, his family ran a grocery store in the Mississippi Delta. He always knew that he was going to run a business. In fact, he believes very strongly that the whole purpose of a business is to make money. He says that he has one conversation, frequently, with managers and employees at every level of his company. It goes like this. Make sure whatever we do makes money. The first question we should ask is, is this going to make us money? Job security happens when we are making money. In other words, Martin was always interested in generating income. He also preferred to own the business himself.

Another leadership attribute that can influence basic business model choices relates to deeply held values. Sometimes your values will stop you from doing certain things, even if those things would be profitable. Other times your values will take you in positive directions. As the child of Chinese immigrants, Martin was always very sensitive to diversity issues and this concern has been reflected in his hiring decisions from the beginning. He brags that his company includes people from all over the world, a factor that surely has contributed to his ability to bring talented engineers and designers to a small southern town. Finally, on a simpler level, the entrepreneur's particular skills and capabilities have a strong influence on how a business model can work. As the next section shows, Martin's electrical engineering skills have certainly played a role in his business.

Key Resources could include people, technology (inventions, patents), products, facilities, equipment, and even things such as established brands, which you can use to create something of value for a customer. These resources may be owned, purchased, or acquired through partnerships.

Although MFJ employs several talented product designers, the major resource related to the company's innovation ability is Martin himself. With his engineering background, he knows how to design products, and, as a ham radio lover, he has an intuitive idea about what to design. He also maintains frequent contact with customers, through attending conferences and giving speeches. He listens to his customers and responds with offerings.

Key Processes include the capabilities needed to make and sell your product.[4] These may include recurrent tasks such as training, research and development, manufacturing, budgeting, planning, sales, marketing, and service. Again, these may be carried out internally or outsourced to partners. Key processes also include a company's rules, metrics, and norms.[5]

One very important key process at MFJ is its approach to manufacturing. The company strives to make everything it can make by itself in order to keep costs low. The firm is fully vertically integrated with all the appropriate machines and equipment.

In addition, the company sells its products through a nationwide network of dealers, as well as an online catalog. Martin and his team also attend ham fests and trade shows to promote their products and meet with customers.

The Profit Formula, according to Johnson, Christensen, and Hagerman,[6] is the blueprint that defines how your company will create value for itself. Understanding your revenue flows is the first step of building this blue print. After that, it is essential to keep a close eye on your profit margins, overhead, breakeven volume, and resource velocity.

Martin understands the importance of cash flow and, particularly, the importance of keeping the cost of sales down. The biggest problem many companies have is that their cost of sales is way too high, he says. This kills everybody.

He keeps his overhead low by operating out of old metal buildings. As an engineer who finds beauty in an electrical circuit, he has little appreciation of aesthetics. He runs his life the same way. He will occasionally buy his wife a new Lexus, but he takes the old one.

Customer Value Proposition. Value propositions explain how your product or service provides value to the customer. Value may be built into actual product or service features, into the channel or delivery system, the brand, and even the pricing mechanism. You can think of it as a package of deliverables. Taken together, these elements lay the groundwork for the total customer experience.

MFJ's value proposition is to provide customers with a broad array of quality ham radio products, which are sold all over the world by a network of over 200 dealers, and an online catalog. Here is what the company has to say on its website:[7]

- MFJ's slogan, "Making Quality Affordable," has been well received in the ham radio community. The niche of the market was captured by offering quality accessory products at low prices.
- Constantly changing and constantly improving, MFJ and its subsidiaries have managed to stay on top of their share of the market by a generous customer service policy and listening to what the customer wants.
- MFJ offers a one year unconditional warranty called the "NO MATTER WHAT" warranty. MFJ will replace or repair a customer's MFJ unit (at MFJ's option) for one complete year. A technical help support line is also offered toll-free for customers needing help or advice with a ham radio project.

Evaluating the Business Model Foundation—Feasibility and Viability

So far, I have described the logic behind MFJ's basic business model. I pointed out earlier that, in a start-up, this model begins as a hypothesis that must be tested. The first two tests are to determine whether the idea is feasible and whether it is viable.

When someone asks if your business model is feasible, they want to know if it can actually be done.[8] Is it realistic? Is the technology available to consistently deliver the promised benefits to consumers?[9] There are many factors that can make a business model unfeasible. Let's consider resources, for instance. Recently, I worked with a group of people who were interested in setting up a wood pellet plant in a small town where land was cheap and the supply of wood was bountiful. In this case, feasibility was problematic because there was no access to rail or water transportation to move the product cheaply to a port.

For Martin Jue, feasibility was not a problem. He had been building electrical circuitry since he was 16 years old. His first product was a high selectivity filter that would enable a receiver to separate one Morse code signal from scores of other signals that were being transmitted over the radio airwaves. He designed it himself using a new technology that allowed him to build it so cheaply that no one else could do it. Then he ran a 2 × 2 advertisement in the now-defunct Ham Radio Magazine (it was full of engineering, technical jargon, he said.). He sold 5,000 in a couple of years, proving the feasibility of the business, but, certainly, this was not enough volume to live on.

A model is viable if you can show that there are enough customers out there willing to buy our product at a price that covers expected costs and generates a profit[10] For someone like Martin, who is interested in generating an income, the actual question is: can you make a living doing it? Answering this question requires a real understanding of who the customers will be and how they will get access to the product. It also requires having a good idea about appropriate price points and cost structures. In fact, it makes sense to say that the whole point of working out your business model is to ensure that your idea will be viable.

The likelihood that your product will be viable is greatly enhanced by being passionate about the industry you are entering. If you are part of it, then you get what the customers want. And you know how to talk to them. Based on the experience with his first product, Martin learned that his customers really wanted something "they could just use…something in boxes." So he got the boxes at Radio Shack and took it up a notch. This time he got a toll-free Watts line and added a couple more products. He ran a full page ad in QST magazine and he sold more in one month than he had in the previous year.

This experiment addressed the viability question. Now he had an understanding of the size of the market, what customers wanted, and how to get access to them. His business model appeared to be viable.

In their book, Blank and Dorf say that the goal of business modeling is to find a repeatable, scalable model.[11] Moreover, the primary value of a start-up is to validate its business model hypothesis. To be feasible, a model has to work; that is, you have to show that you can craft an offering that does what it is supposed to do when customers use it. To be viable, you have to show that customers will actually buy it. As Martin Jue says, the key is selling something. Or to put it another way, the key is having enough customers who are willing to buy that you can cover your costs and earn a profit.

MFJ's Business Model Differentiators

Feasibility and viability are important to building a business model and getting your new company off the ground. However, additional considerations must be made to ensure that the model will be sustainable over time. Key among these is finding ways to differentiate the firm from competitors and provide superior value to customers. Figure 4.2 shows MFJ's differentiators.

The key factors separating MFJ from other competitors include both Martin's ability to lead the development of innovative new products and, at the same time, to keep costs low. MFJ's innovation capabilities stem

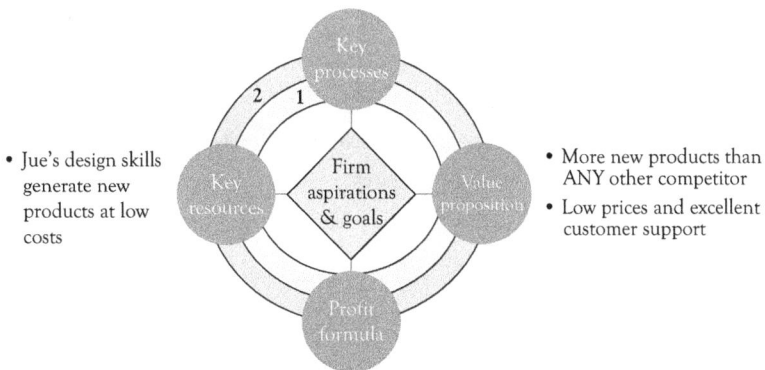

Figure 4.2. M.F.J's differentiated business model.

from several factors, including Martin's personal interest in the hobby, his connection with his customers, and his electrical engineering skills.

As I pointed out earlier, Martin has been a ham radio fan since he was a child. If you look in his back yard, he has wires draped across his deck and tacked to his house. If you visit his office, you can see his collection of radios that has been accumulating for years. He gets it. In addition, he and his team of managers like to go to hamfests. They travel from Mississippi to events as far away as New Hampshire, Texas, Florida, and Oregon. The hamfests allow MFJ leaders to meet customers in their local arenas and to keep in touch with their needs.

Another way that Martin keeps in touch with his customers is through the company website. Although the website is very technical, it is designed to appeal to the serious amateur radio operator. Martin personally writes the descriptions of many different products, and he carefully hones his words to reach out to his customers. He wants them to read each description and say only one thing—I'll buy that. Customers can also post reviews of each product. More recently, a Facebook page has been created and conversations occur there as well.

Martin's personality and background are also instrumental in his passion for keeping costs low. He is fanatical about cutting out excess costs by building everything possible in-house. And, as I mentioned earlier, the facilities are certainly bare bones. When you combine these capabilities, you can see why MFJ actually provides better value than competitors do. The company's value proposition is based on offering superior value to ham radio operators by offering the broadest array of products on the market, at great prices, and with excellent support by a firm that understands hams.

As Martin says, the company designs and sells more new products continually than anyone else in the business. The MFJ value proposition is part of a complex business model that is both low cost and differentiated, based on its continual innovation and introduction of new products and its low-cost operating style.

A Note on Integrated Business Models

As I've already mentioned, MFJ uses a vertically integrated model. As mentioned in Chapter 2, this was once the dominant form of business model among manufacturers. However, over the past half century, many industries have undergone fundamental changes and a breaking up of these integrated business models has occurred.[12]

In recent years, many integrated business models have been split into smaller and smaller segments as new specialized businesses have been created. As a result, vertically integrated companies like MFJ now face speedy new competitors who specialize in just one step of the value chain (and do it better or cheaper). Another new breed of competitor is one who orchestrates a whole network of suppliers in creating a customer offering. Each supplier contributes a different step to the final product.

These kinds of changes are not only creating new businesses and new markets, but also causing formerly separate industries to converge. Consider mobile phones, computers, and televisions. Changes in technology, government deregulation, and managerial creativity are all accelerating this trend.[13] These kinds of changes are also making it easier for new entrepreneurs to start their companies. You don't have to do your own manufacturing any more. Just find a partner. Or find several partners.

What About the Future?

The integrated business model configuration has worked very well for MFJ. For this company, vertical integration has helped keep costs low and speed products to market. In fact, MFJ's business model has sustained the firm for 40 years. This is clearly a success story for Martin and his team.

Looking forward from here, however, leads to some difficult questions. The big one is this—What might happen to the firm without Martin? He is the key to MFJ's differentiation and competitive advantage in the market place. Without his influence, the entire model might come apart at the seams. Martin believes that it would take several different people to replace his unique position within the firm. This is the next issue that he will have to confront to sustain his company for the longer term.

Summary and Conclusions

In this chapter, I used the foundation and differentiated business model lenses to show how a company can create superior value for its customers through good business model design and hard work. Like Joel Bomgar, Martin Jue was able to put this model together because he had an intuitive understanding of his customers and their needs. Also like Joel, Martin was an engineer who could bring his product ideas to life. But with Martin, we saw one more thing, and that was his clear focus on building a business that would make money and provide him and his family, and his employees, with a good life. He never lost this focus. In fact, even today, he preaches this lesson to young entrepreneurs whenever he gets the chance.

The next chapter looks at a very different business model based on a very different way of providing value. The company is called TOMS and the founder is Blake Mykoskie.

CHAPTER 5

TOMS Shoes

Selling a Vision

As we saw in Chapters 3 and 4, planning your business model should begin with an in-depth understanding of your customers and their current concerns. As Johnson, Christensen, and Kagleman note, "it all starts with thinking about the opportunity to satisfy a real customer who needs a job done."[1] Both Joel Bomgar and Martin Jue knew their customers very well.

But what happens when your business idea is based on something else? Like the belief that you can make the world a better place. The question to be addressed in this chapter is: Can you build a successful business model around selling a vision? And if so, how do you ensure that your customers will continue to be part of the vision?

TOMS Shoes

I first heard about TOMS Shoes' founder, Blake Mycoskie, when he gave a talk at my university in 2010. The students turned out in droves to hear him. This was a surprise to me because I had been working hard to bring speakers to campus that would resonate with the student body. We brought in famous generals, nationally known political pundits, and cable television news experts, but never did we get the response that Blake Mykoskie got.

Since its founding in 2006, this company has grown quickly into a phenomenon. By 2012, it had sold over 2 million pairs of shoes and given away an equal amount using Mykoskie's "buy-one give-one business model."[2] With this model, TOMS appears to be the perfect exemplar of a vision-driven business, or one that is striving to produce a positive effect on the world. The first interesting thing to think about in this story is how Blake came to put this idea together.

Blake Mycoskie was 29 years old when he started his business. Before TOMS, Blake, a native of Texas, had already started five businesses. His first was a successful campus laundry service, which he later sold. Between business ventures, Blake competed in the CBS primetime series, *The Amazing Race*. With his sister, Paige, Blake traveled the world and came within minutes of winning the $1 million grand prize. This experience in putting together companies, as well as the publicity he got from being in a T.V. show were both important in explaining his ability to put such a successful start-up together so quickly.

A couple of years after *The Amazing Race*, Blake visited Argentina again, for a vacation. While exploring the country, two things happened. First, he met an American woman who was volunteering with an organization that collected shoes from donors and gave them to kids in need. She told him that many kids lacked shoes, even in relatively well-developed countries such as Argentina, an absence that complicated their attempts to go to school, and also exposed them to a wide range of diseases.[3] What interested Blake, in addition to the idea of delivering shoes to kids, was the fact that the efforts were currently hampered by lack of control over the supply of shoes to deliver. The organization relied on donations that were hit or miss, in terms of timing, size, and amounts.

The second thing that happened was Blake's discovery of a traditional Peruvian shoe called the *alpargata*, a soft casual shoe worn all around the country.[4] He thought that the style and feel of the shoe might go over well in the United States. Thus, he came up with his new business idea:

> "Why not create a for-profit business to help provide shoes for these children? Why not come up with a solution that guaranteed a constant flow of shoes, not just whenever kind people were able to make a donation? In other words, maybe the solution was in entrepreneurship, not charity."[5]

And so the idea was born to create a business model that revolved around making a new kind of *alpargata* to sell in the Unitd States, and, for every pair sold, to give a pair to a child.[6] It took some research, but eventually Mycoskie found a Peruvian shoe maker to put together a couple hundred pairs of his new design. The shoes were named TOMS—shoes for tomorrow.

After flying back to California, with a duffle bag full of shoes, he talked to friends about how to sell them, and identified a top Los Angeles clothing store, American Rag, to sell his shoes. The owner loved the story as well as the shoes, and it wasn't long before a fashion writer for the *Los Angeles Times* heard the story and loved it too. On the day that her article appeared, the TOMS' website had received 2,200 orders. Since there were only 160 pairs of shoes remaining in the duffle bag, Blake hired three student interns who called everyone on the list and told them they would have to wait for a while until the shoes could be made (he lost one order). Then he raced back to Argentina and to figure out how to manufacture more. It was about then that *Vogue* ran a big story, and stories began popping up everywhere. He sold 10,000 pairs working out of his apartment that first summer. The rest is history.

The next section describes some of the logic behind the design of TOMS' differentiated business model. The interesting thing here is that TOMS did not start out as a basic shoe company. In fact, it was never a basic shoe company. From the first moment, it has always been a company that gives a pair of shoes to a child for every pair of shoes sold. In other words, this is a case where the business model was differentiated right from the start. There is no real reason to consider the foundation separately from the differentiators. They were built simultaneously in support of the buy-one-give-one idea. Thus, we can begin with the differentiated business model lens shown in Figure 5.1.

Key Resources and Processes. To get his company up and going quickly, Blake drew on his personal network of friends and acquaintances to raise money and to find outlets for selling his shoes. He sold the business he was currently running (online driver education instruction) to his partners and then invested a half million dollars of his own money into his new venture. As sales grew, his ability to form partnerships remained an important means of carrying out the firm's operations in a low-cost way. For instance, the company delivers its shoes through partnerships with charitable and religious organizations in the countries of choice. Volunteers can also sign up to participate in the shoe drops on the company's website.

A major part of the business model is that the company does not have a marketing budget. It buys no advertising, relying on word of mouth, viral marketing, and social media. Obviously, Mycoskie has excelled at getting free publicity for TOMS by telling its story in many different venues,

- No advertising budget
- Manufacturing in three countries
- Partner non profits deliver shoes

Key processes

2 1

- Network of friends and partners
- Volunteers
- Free publicity

Key resources

Blake's aspirations & goals

Value proposition

- Trendy, cute shoes
- Customers feel good for helping others

Profit formula

- Purchase price covers two pairs of shoes
- Low cost of manufacturing
- Inexpensive materials

- Four prior startups
- "Amazing Race" fame
- Vision of helping children
- $500,000 cash

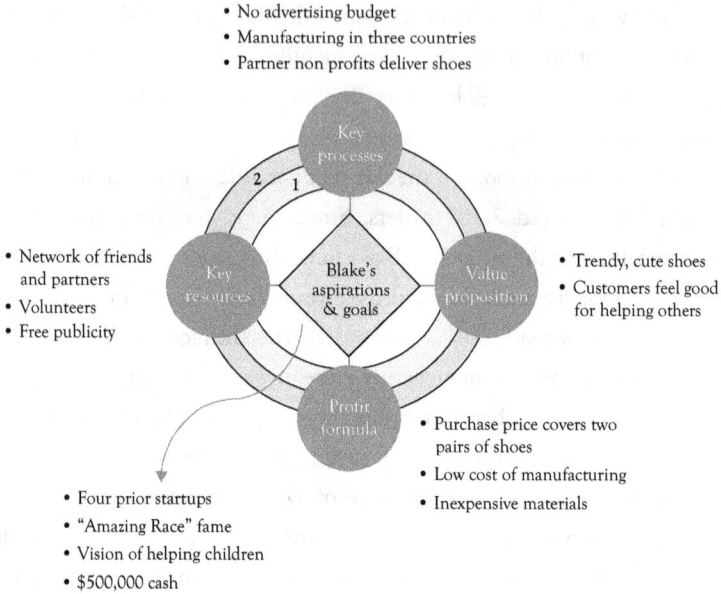

Figure 5.1. TOMS' differentiated business model.

giving speeches, attending conferences, and appearing online. In addition to the stories mentioned earlier, the company has been written up in many magazines and newspapers, and there are stories and videos all over the web. Celebrities are often seen wearing TOMS shoes or wearing no shoes on the annual "Day without Shoes" campaign.[7] Clearly, people love this story.

The company headquarters is still in California where about 90 people are employed. Manufacturing is outsourced to facilities in Argentina, Ethiopia, and China, another decision that helps to keep costs low. According to TOMS' website, the company requires its factories to operate under sound labor conditions, pay fair wages, and follow the International Labor Standards set by the International Labor Organization. Also, according to its website, it strives to manufacture at least some shoes in the countries in which it gives shoes.[8]

Profit Margin Considerations. Since its inception in 2006, TOMS has given away over two million pairs of shoes to children in 40 developing countries. The company's canvas slip-on shoes—the same type it often donates—now sell for $45 to $135 a pair in over 500 different retailers ranging from Nordstrom and Neiman Marcus to independent shoe stores.

TOMS profit formula is based on the premise that the purchase price actually covers two pairs of shoes, one for the customer and one for a child in need. Also, as this discussion has shown so far, the company keeps its costs in check by using volunteers and partners as well as receiving a great deal of free advertising. In addition, the shoes are made of inexpensive materials. Although the costs are not made public, one estimate suggests that you could make the basic canvas shoes (which retail at about $50.00 a pair) for somewhere between $5 and $9 and that the smaller child's pairs that are given away for even less.[9] This lends some credence to the idea that the firm is quite profitable.

Customer Value Proposition. The real force behind TOMS business model, however, is that when customers buy TOMS shoes, they get both the trendy shoes and the story. They are buying an opportunity to feel that they are doing good through their purchase. In the short run, this value proposition has been so successful that the company has added several other products to its lineup and it has inspired other entrepreneurs to try similar business models. Mycoskie also states that he chose the publisher for his book based on its willingness to agree to a buy-one-book give-one-book arrangement.[10]

With regard to the shoes themselves, reactions vary. On the cost side, TOMS shoes are not particularly beautiful; they are made from canvas and plastic, and they have little arch support. They are also pricy. On the benefit side, TOMS shoes are very trendy and recognizable, they come in a variety of bright colors, and they are easily accessible at many stores and online.

The TOMS' business model shows that we do not just buy things to resolve our immediate problems. We will also buy things that we believe will make the world a better place, or that might make ourselves a little better person. According to the Cone Cause Evolution study, 80 percent of Americans are likely to switch brands, if comparable in price and quality, to one that supports a social cause.[11] It seems that many customers find value in purchasing products or services that are associated with causes they believe in.

Firm Leadership and Logic. Blake Mycoskie was not initially driven by a vision to bring shoes to poor children across the world. He was an entrepreneur who had started five businesses, and he stumbled upon this idea during his travels to South America. Although he has attributed his desire to help others to the fact that his dad is a doctor and his mom wrote a cookbook based on healthy recipes, he was not out there looking for a way to help children. Rather, he stumbled upon the idea. And from there, he built it into his business model.

David Teece suggests that business model pioneers often possess—or develop—an understanding of some deep truth about the fundamental needs of consumers and how competitors are not satisfying those needs.[12] It was certainly easy to see why Joel Bomgar understood the frustrations of computer technicians and Martin Jue understood amateur radio operators. It is more difficult to understand how Blake Mycoskie knew that customers would be excited about paying a higher price to purchase their own shoes in order to give shoes to children. Obviously, his hypothesis was spot on. And, in addition, he had the know-how to build an organization that could satisfy that need.

Clearly, not everyone could have implemented the buy-one give-one business model with as much success as Blake Mycoskie. He already knew how to build a profitable business and he had a half million dollars of his own to invest, so he didn't have to raise a lot of cash. Also, consider the publicity he gained in his stint on the popular television show, *The Amazing Race*. He was not only able to take advantage of his celebrity status but also easily able to contact other well-known people. He was quickly noticed by the press that was keen to tell his story and provided him with a wealth of free publicity. And, his shoe sales took off immediately, showing him the power of the vision he was selling. His biggest challenge was to scale the business up quickly enough to avoid losing momentum.

Like Joel Bomgar and Martin Jue, Blake was and is a key part of the business model. Even today, he calls himself "chief shoe giver" instead of "chief executive officer."[13]

The Toms Model Is an Orchestrator Model

Although most people focus on the buy-one-give-one aspect of the TOMS' business model, I would describe that facet of the model as a key differentiator. The underlying configuration of the TOMS model is best captured by the term "Orchestrator Model" since the company coordinates activities in a network of suppliers.[14] Orchestrators focus on one or a few core steps of the value chain, while outsourcing and coordinating the others.[15] Competitive advantage is derived from superior coordination capabilities that give them access to all needed assets and access to the entire value chain.[16]

Interestingly, Nike, the famous athletic shoe company, is another highly successful orchestrator business in the shoe industry, founded by the 26-year-old Phil Knight in the late 1960s. Nike's success has been based not only on the quality of its shoes, but also on its highly popular advertisements and endorsements of well-known athletes beginning with Michael Jordan. It has built a cult-like following over the years by understanding how to turn shoes into a status symbol. Like TOMS, most of Nike's shoes are manufactured in Asia. Unfortunately, the company has been criticized many times for using independent contractors who mistreat workers and pay them poorly.

TOMS has also been criticized for manufacturing in China but not because of poor conditions in its suppliers' manufacturing facilities. In fact, as noted earlier, the company is careful to discuss, on its website, these conditions and the steps that it takes to protect workers. The real case against TOMS is that its business model may do more harm than good in the countries it is supposedly trying to help. The argument is that by bringing free shoes to children in poor countries, there will be less opportunity for shoe manufacturers there to make a living and there will be increased dependence on foreign kindness.[17] If these complaints get louder or more frequent, some buyers may change their minds about the value of their purchase. To sustain itself in the long run, the company may have to begin assisting communities with manufacturing their own shoes. As a recent *Forbes* article pointed out:

> "Toms could actually strengthen their business model by moving *away* from charity and toward scalable manufacturing and production practices that better monetize Toms by pulling former 'charity cases' into an actual productive economic relationship with Toms and with one another."[18]

The debate is still on as to whether TOMS is doing good in the world. To sustain sales over the long term, the company not only has to convince customers that its actions are positive, but also has to ensure that they are. Nike, for instance, has a social responsibility division with over 150 people in it and it is still being criticized for conditions in its Indonesian supplier firms. [19] To be successful as a global orchestrator, the company must pay careful attention to the selection of suppliers and practice effective governance.

Sustainability Concerns and Responses

Criticisms of its international shoe drop approach are not the only threats to TOMS' sustainability. Here at home, TOMS is vulnerable both to competitors in the shoe business and to those nonprofit and charitable organizations promising to do good things.

On the shoe side, Sketchers has already made a direct run at TOMS with a line of simple canvas shoes named BOBS. They look a lot like TOMS shoes. In fact, Sketchers even promises to donate a pair to a child in need whenever a pair is bought.[20] However, the Sketchers shoes are so similar, and the promise so clearly copied, that customer reactions have been minimal.

Yet, shoes are fashion items and trends change quickly. Moreover, there are hundreds of shoe companies out there with wide variations in design and quality. To stay in tune with consumer tastes, the company will have to innovate constantly. In addition to its basic canvas slip-on, the company is now offering the bota (ankle boot) and cordones (sneaker with laces) for both sexes. Recently, it has increased its shoe lines to include new VEGAN TOMS (made of 70% of plastic recycled bottles and 30% hemp…) as well as wedding TOMS for those who prefer a casual option in that setting. The company is also making some shoes from pesticide-free cotton canvas, and using recycled rubber scraps in the soles. All of these innovations indicate that the company is aware that selling shoes, actual shoes, is critical for the buy-one give-one model to be sustainable in the long haul. And to sell shoes, the firm will have to make sure they stay trendy and stylish and that they provide the benefits that people are looking for when they buy shoes.

On the feel-good side, the big question is: Will customers get bored with giving shoes? What is to stop them from moving to the next opportunity to feel good about themselves?

To sustain interest, the company is continually innovating in terms of the way it does good. Although the company still mainly gives the canvas shoe to children, it has developed shoes with thick rubber soles for those who live in monsoon areas as well as orthopedic boots for Ethiopian children who suffer from a disease called elephant foot.[21] In addition to adding more products such as TOMS' tee shirts to the buy-one-give-one offer, it is also experimenting with new ways of helping people. For instance, when you buy a pair of TOMS' eyeglasses, a child in Nepal or Cambodia or Tibet may get a pair of glasses, or may receive eye surgery to correct the problem.

All of these moves are designed to connect to the customer and differentiate the TOMS brand from competition. If TOMS can maintain its status as the exemplar in the buy-one-give-one category, then it may be able to hold on to its following. To do so, it will have to continue to innovate, but must also strive to be authentic. According to Aakers:

> "The authentic brand is perceived to be real rather than phony, a brand that will deliver the category or subcategory quality, a leader rather than a copier, one that took risks to create the defining innovation, and reliable and trustworthy."[22]

Authenticity requires making difficult decisions and doing the right thing. However, just like the product attributes described earlier, authenticity is determined by the customers. In the end, they are the ones making the determination.

Building Customer Relationships

The ultimate key to TOMS' sustainability will be whether it can continue to convince its customers that they are part of a worthwhile movement, and that through their purchases, they will be part of something that is good for the world. To think more clearly about involving their customer base, Mycoskie and his leadership team should include their customer base as a part of the resources and find novel ways to include them in rebuilding their brand and their actual activities for the future. Figure 5.2 looks at TOMS through the adaptive business model lens, which includes the customers as part of the business model.

Figure 5.2 lists some of the questions that TOMS' leadership should consider in order to sustain or renew the model in the future. As the next paragraphs show, the company is engaging in some key activities that are aimed at building and nurturing its customer relationships and incorporating customers in its vision.

For instance, TOMS is doing several things that would seem to be aimed at building a sense of community with its customers.[23] Social media is heavily used to provide a link to customers. Each pair of TOMS shoes now comes with a blue and white flag card. Customers can take their pictures wearing the shoes and upload them to the "THIS IS HOW WE WEAR THEM" campaign featured on the company's website, plus Facebook and Twitter. In addition, Style your Sole parties are available to

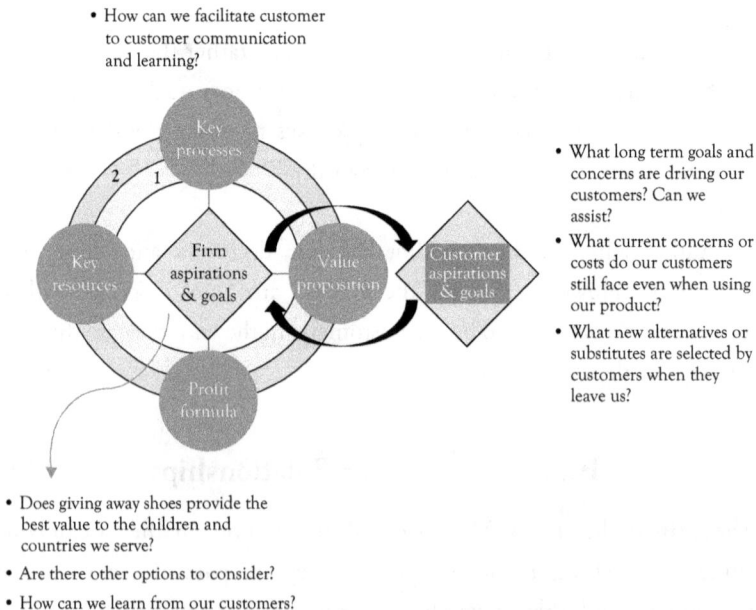

Figure 5.2. TOMS' adaptive business model.

groups. You paint blank white shoes (and you get a 10% discount if you buy more than 25 pairs).

More importantly, perhaps, are activities aimed at involving the customers in TOMS' philanthropic efforts.[24] For instance, the company sponsors a variety of activities for college students and others.

- TOMS campus clubs—service clubs are formed at high schools and colleges with a mission of helping children in need.
- TOMS hires interns (called Agents of Change and Vagabonds) to take on projects and promote the shoes. The company looks for people who truly believe in what TOMS stands for.
- Campus groups can get a DVD about TOMS and use it to facilitate discussions about the company's activities and other opportunities to get involved.

While these steps are clearly moving in the right direction, I would argue that the next step should involve TOMS' staff in listening and learning from these discussions with customers. Finding the right ways to help the world is not easy. The more voices you can get into the conversation, the better your chances of choosing the right path.

Mycoskie calls his business, Philanthropic Capitalism. The company makes a profit, but it incorporates philanthropy into its business model and strategy. According to Mykoskie: "It's important that we're profitable, and this year we will be for the first time, because that's the only way you can truly have sustainability. Ultimately, I'm trying to create something that's going to be here long after I'm gone."[25]

If this is to occur, the question that Mycoskie and his company will have to ask, again and again, is the following: What is the "deep truth" about what these customers *really* value and how can the company develop its value proposition to continue to satisfy those needs?[26]

Summary and Conclusions

This chapter has looked at the way one entrepreneur, Blake Mycoskie, built a business model around a customer value proposition that appeals to customers' higher level goals. The vision he offered was so compelling to customers that he was able to reduce the costs of marketing in his business model and cover the costs of giving away shoes to children. Sales took off immediately and are still going strong. Currently, the company is trying to strengthen its relationship with its customers, and is continually adding new shoes, as well as other products, including glasses, in an effort to stay in tune with customers' tastes and stay ahead of competitors.

In the long run, however, the company will have to confront ethical questions about its policies of bringing free shoes into the Third World countries. As the Nike example shows, these questions will get louder and stronger as the company continues to grow. In addition, new concerns are likely to arise given the company's status as a global orchestrator business. As Robert Reich says, companies like this are no longer really "American" companies. They've become global networks that design, make, buy, and sell things wherever around the world it's most profitable for them to do so.[27]

For TOMS' business model to be sustainable in the long run, customers will have to continue buying TOMS shoes and apparel and they will have to continue to believe that by purchasing from TOMS, they are part of something that is good for the world. In other words, they must become part of the business model. In addition, customer input may be crucial to revising and renewing TOMS' model over time in a way that fits with changing values and societal norms.

In the next chapter, I tell the story of a firm that chose not to listen to its customers. In fact, it is a company that is well known in a positive way for its powerful business model—Netflix.

CHAPTER 6

Netflix Cancels the Value Exchange Agreement

In Chapter 5, I talked about some of the steps that TOMS is taking to sustain its value relationship with customers. As Figure 6.1 shows, the value exchange relationship is both an agreement and a relationship between firms and their customers. A strong relationship is one where both parties are satisfied with the outcome of the exchanged values, whether these outcomes are social or economic. Exchange theorists also contend that all relationships require some time and effort on the part of the parties involved.[1] In fact, once established, this relationship is so important to your company that I believe that you should build it into your business model.

The reason why you need to focus on this relationship in your business modeling efforts is because you are never in total control. According to social exchange theorists, people review and weigh their relationships in terms of costs and rewards.[2] If your customers determine that the benefits of purchasing your products do not outweigh the costs, or that someone else is providing superior benefits at the same cost, they will abandon you and move on to another provider. Netflix learned this lesson the hard way when it angered its most loyal customers by abruptly announcing a radical change in its pricing policies for DVDs by mail and by streaming.

Netflix's original business model, unlimited DVDs by mail for a subscription price of about $9.99 per month, is a textbook example of a model that raised the bar on customer value and transformed an entire industry. Once Netflix came on the scene, it wasn't long before the former industry leader, Blockbuster, went bankrupt. Netflix offered a wider variety of films, at a lower price, delivered to your door. Eventually, it introduced instant streaming of a smaller selection of films as a free addition. It was a

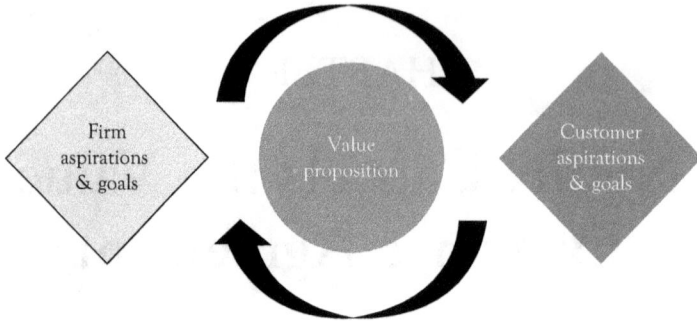

Figure 6.1. Value exchange relationship.

winning combination and one that customers appreciated. The firm had a large and growing base of loyal customers.

In July of 2011, the company announced that it was splitting the streaming business from the DVD business and converting them into separate divisions. Now, customers could purchase unlimited streaming only at $7.99 a month and unlimited DVDs at $7.99, resulting in a $15.98-per-month subscription charge for both. That resulted in a sudden 60 percent price hike for its current customers. This sudden change shattered the value exchange agreement. Customers revolted. Within 3 months, the company lost at least 800,000 customers.[3] Stock prices plummeted. A year later, they have fallen even further.[4]

What Netflix failed to realize is that at this stage of its evolution, its customers are now a key part of its business model. According to strategy guru, Gary Hamel, value creation and value capture occur within a value network, which can include suppliers, partners, distributors, and coalitions that extend the company's resources. This network also includes the firm's customers.[5]

If Netflix had considered its current customers to be part of its model, it might have avoided making decisions that angered them. One important purpose of a business model is to help managers consider the logic and internal consistency of their strategic decisions.[6] Business models can help managers avoid making ill-conceived decisions by forcing them to consider a range of decisions holistically.[7] This is the utility of the business model as a conceptual tool.

Although Netflix implemented its business model foundations and also differentiated itself brilliantly for years, I contend that it never paid much attention to its value exchange agreement with customers. Instead, once new competitors began to emerge, it revised its original model and value propositions, with too little effort on sustaining the customer relationship. As a result, the company's reputation was ruined, and its credibility shattered.[8] On the day that the new pricing scheme was announced, over 4,100 comments were posted on Netflix's own blog page, most of them glaringly negative.[9] Moreover, thousands more negative comments were posted on Twitter and Facebook.

Yet, if we consider the underlying economics of the fundamental Netflix business model, we can see why the company wanted to make the change. The lesson here is that once customers buy into your value proposition, you can't just arbitrarily change the deal. In the next section, we look more closely at the logic behind Netflix's decision to change, and what it might have done to sustain its relationship with customers.

A Winning Business Model Versus Forces for Change

Let's review Netflix's business model as of 2010 and consider the factors that led to this change. With regard to key resources, the company had built a huge library of over 75,000 films on DVDs obtained through partnerships and agreements with a broad variety of movie studios and television networks. Its key processes were innovative and cutting edge from its red mailing envelopes, which accomodated both customer delivery and returns, to its easy-to-navigate website.

A key process in the winning Netflix model was the recommendation algorithm, which leads customers to a wide array of films based on their past preferences. This algorithm not only helped customers find good movies, but also helped the company leverage its film library by reducing demand for currently popular titles.[10] Interestingly, the company acquired the algorithm by offering the Netflix Prize—a million dollars to the programmer or team who could develop an algorithm that would meet specified accuracy goals based on customers' past preferences.[11] This is an excellent example of open innovation, which involves bringing in new ideas from outside your company.[12]

We should also consider the company's profit situation prior to its sudden pricing change in 2011. That year, Netflix had over 22 million subscribers.[13]

As I mentioned earlier, it was charging its customers $9.99 per month for the basic, unlimited mail delivery, and streaming combination. And it earned $320 million profit on $2.1 billion in revenue based on providing both of these services.[14]

It was about that time that new entrants such as Hulu and Amazon Prime were coming on the scene. These competitors provided video streaming only and did not have to carry the large infrastructure needed to store and mail the DVDs. Although it cost more to buy the rights to stream a film than to buy the DVD and rent it, Netflix believed that streaming was going to become the new norm. And it needed more money from customers if it was going to spend more to lease additional materials for its streaming service.[15] In addition, getting rid of the mailing infrastructure could help balance those higher costs. So it began to look at its profit margin and its overall cost structure in a different way.

To complicate matters more, with the new entrants coming along, the television and movie studios now had more distributors to choose from, which increased their power to increase prices. And those with their own cable networks were starting to see Netflix as a competitor, since some customers were quitting cable in favor of renting movies through Netflix. For Netflix, this meant that the industry was in flux and that deals were getting tougher. Early in 2011, it lost its Disney partnership. Later on, it lost Sony.

As Figure 6.2 shows, using the differentiated business model lens, the new pricing structure that Netflix announced in April of 2011 was really just the tip of the iceberg in terms of the real changes to come in its business model. The new structure was designed to attract streaming-only customers, and possibly to reduce DVD customers. The problem was that the old arrangement—unlimited DVDs and streaming—had given its current customers the best of all worlds, a huge library of DVD selections, with some extra goodies available by streaming. To customers, it seemed that Netflix ripped away this value with seemingly no regard for their preferences. This huge reduction in value led to a huge customer revolt.

In the months following the customer rebellion, Reed Hasting, the CEO of Netflix, stated that he had been guilty of overconfidence and of "moving too quickly." But he said he still believed—as do most investors and analysts—that Netflix's future lay not in DVDs but in streaming over the Internet. "We still need to move quickly in streaming," he said.[16]

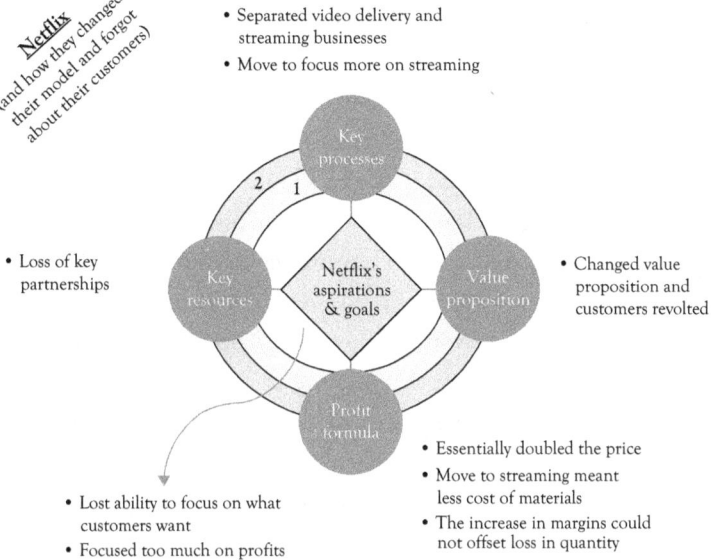

Figure 6.2. Netflix changes its business model.

When asked if he had discussed the change with customers, prior to its announcement, he said he was not sure whether the plan had been presented to customer focus groups before it was made public. According to a New York Times article, "Mr. Hastings said he assumed it had been. But he said he did not recall what those focus groups had said about the plan."[17]

What Hastings forgot was that the company's initial success in establishing the Netflix DVD delivery model was always based on what it learned from its customers. The Netflix prize elicited brilliant ideas from software teams far and wide. And then, using this crowd-sourcing algorithm, the firm had strengthened its relationship with customers by using their past choices to influence their future purchases.

Hastings was undoubtedly right that Netflix needs to move into streaming video. However, he may have been wrong about the need to do it so fast. He seemed to dismiss the value of his relationships with millions of customers when actually they would have been happy to help him figure out how to make the move forward. When streaming was first introduced on a limited basis, customers were getting additional value—instant streaming combined with a deep reservoir of movie titles on DVD. In fact, the gradual addition allowed customers to learn how to add the hardware they needed to build their systems. The company could have continued this evolution and even allowed their customers to generate feedback and new ideas, perhaps even with regard to how to change the pricing mechanisms in ways that would still benefit users. Perhaps the firm could have offered different pricing options, at least for some period of time.

There are many reasons why you should include customers in your business modeling decisions. Because they always have the choice to leave, you need to find ways to nurture the relationship and adapt your offering to meet their evolving needs. A simple step is to continually ask them for input on how you can do a better job.[18] In addition, once you have them, you may realize that they are an actual resource; for instance, letting them promote movies to each other might increase rentals of some films. Finally, if you are sincere in your efforts to learn, you may find that customers can actually help to generate new value propositions, attract new paying customers, or generate new sources of revenues.[19]

Netflix was famous for its algorithm that captured customer preferences and recommended films you might like, but it has been very slow in using its website to create any kind of conversations or social community. I think it could learn a bit from TOMS here, and other businesses that are greatly benefitting from this kind of customer engagement. Incorporating customers in your business model is more complex, but it opens your eyes to their perspectives and allows you to learn from their behaviors and inputs.

Summary and Conclusion

This chapter reviewed the Netflix business model before and after its customer and stockholders rebelled. The company's development of its DVD by mail model was brilliant, completely changing the game in the video rental industry. When the emergence of new streaming technologies and competitors threatened to disrupt this model, CEO Reed Hastings moved quickly to transform and renew the company's business model, but he did so without attending to the value exchange agreement the firm had established with its customers. As a result, the firm's reputation was damaged.

Yet, Netflix is a large company, with many customers, and today, its customer base is growing again. The mistake discussed here may just be a growing pain or an adolescent stumble in a terribly uncertain competitive environment. Application of an adaptive business model lens might help companies such as Netflix to do a better job of incorporating their customer relationships into their strategic considerations. Customers can be sources of information and learning, possibly making change easier in the future. Learning can be difficult, but whatever it takes, keep learning.

The next chapter looks at Rent-the-Runway, a firm that has applied a Netflix-type model in a very different industry, designer clothing rentals. The interesting part of this story is that the two entrepreneurs who started this business have built in learning and customer relationship development at every opportunity from the very beginning.

CHAPTER 7

Rent the Runway

Changing Customer Behaviors and Industry Norms

When Jennifer Fleiss and Jennifer Hyman started Rent the Runway (RTR) in 2009, they wanted to provide women with "aspirational products from top designers" that they might otherwise not be able to afford.[1] In 2012, the firm has over 3 million customers and is adding about 100,000 new members each month. RTR members typically range from 15- to 35-year-olds.[2]

To use the website, you must first become a member, which is free. This gives you access to over 25,000 dresses and 4,000 accessories in sizes 0–16 with rental prices ranging from approximately $30 to $250. Each rental includes a backup size at no additional cost to ensure fit, and customers can also get a second dress style with their order for an additional $25, plus an optional $5 insurance fee. To return the dresses, you slip them into the enclosed envelope and drop it into the mailbox. It's a lot like the Netflix model, before streaming.

But unlike Netflix, this new company leads the way in incorporating its customers into its business model while, at the same time, using its model to shape customer behavior. RTR is part of an evolving value network that is changing retailing forever, and it will be interesting to see how long this company can ride the wave, and to what extent it will actually lead the way. In such a dynamic situation, competitive threats can emerge suddenly, and from unexpected directions. In this chapter, I first examine the firm's differentiated business model, and then show how it interacts with customers and builds customer relationships by using the adaptive model as a lens. I also explore how RTR's business model and others similar to it are impacting retail in general, and how these new models have potential to add to the woes of many traditional retailers in the next few years.

Building the RTR Customer Value Proposition

Figure 7.1 presents an overview of RTR's start-up approach and its differentiated business model.

Leadership and vision. Jenn Hyman and Jenny Fleiss met on the first day of class when they started Harvard's MBA program after several years of industry experience, Hyman in marketing at Starwood, and Fleiss in finance at Morgan Stanley and Lehman Brothers. They were in their second year of their program when Jenn got the idea for a business after watching her younger sister trying to make up her mind about buying an expensive dress for a wedding.[3] After she and her friend, Jenny, talked about the idea, they decided to go for it. "We had an idea, we thought that it was fun, we decided to start working on it," says Hyman. "We never had a business plan. We pretended that we had a business from the very beginning, as opposed to planning and strategizing as to whether it would work."[4]

To test the idea, they bought a truckload of dresses, with their own money, and offered to rent them to undergraduate students at Harvard and Yale. The students snatched them up.

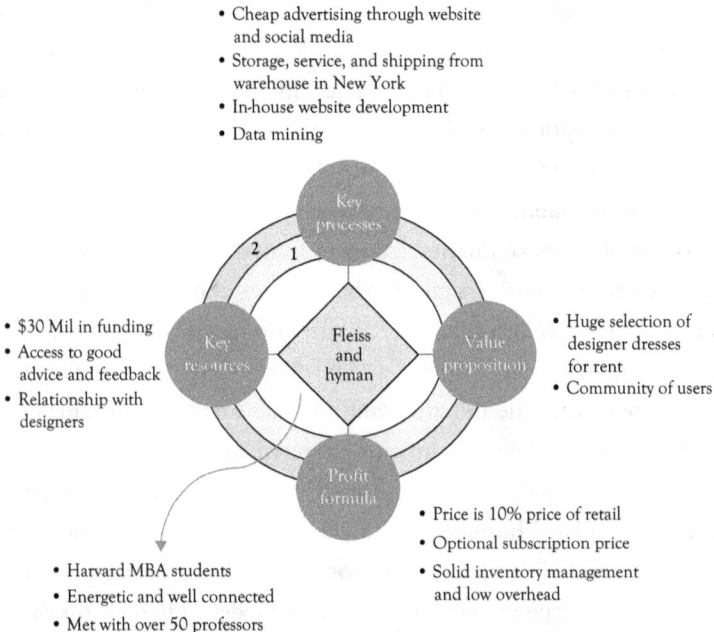

- Cheap advertising through website and social media
- Storage, service, and shipping from warehouse in New York
- In-house website development
- Data mining

Key processes

- $30 Mil in funding
- Access to good advice and feedback
- Relationship with designers

Key resources

Fleiss and hyman

Value proposition

- Huge selection of designer dresses for rent
- Community of users

Profit formula

- Price is 10% price of retail
- Optional subscription price
- Solid inventory management and low overhead

- Harvard MBA students
- Energetic and well connected
- Met with over 50 professors

Figure 7.1. Rent the Runway differentiated model.

"While Ms. Hyman watched, a girl tried on a silver-sequined Tory Burch mini-dress, twirled in front of the mirror and turned to her two friends to exclaim, "Oh my God, I look so hot!" "Her two friends ran to the racks and rented as well," says Ms. Hyman. "We saw the power of women influencing each other."[5]

Once they received their MBAs, they started meeting with designers about the idea. "The first designer we met with was interested, and after that, we jumped right in," says Fleiss. They used the same energy in seeking connections with the media, leveraging their contacts, and meeting with anyone who would respond. Eventually they met a *New York Times* reporter who liked their concept. The story she published drove over 100,000 members to their site in its first week and they exceeded their first year projections in the first month.[6]

After seeking out a venture capitalist, the pair launched the website in November of 2009.[7] Eventually the company raised over $30 million in funding.[8]

Key resources. As Harvard MBA students, Jenn and Jenny had access to many knowledgeable people. In addition to conducting focus groups and running tests, the team met with over 50 professors at Harvard Business School, whether they had taken classes with them or not. They asked for and received a great deal of advice and feedback.[9]

Designers are another key resource. Designers are to RTR what the studios are to Netflix. Without the consent of designers, who are highly selective about their distribution channels, the business model would not have flourished. Luckily, designers embraced the concept as it allowed them to "reach a larger audience and age demographic without jeopardizing the brand."[10]

The company began with 1,000 dresses from 25 designers in the first year. It now has 25,000 dresses from 150 designers, including prominent designers Diane von Furstenberg, Zac Posen, Helmut Lang, Kate Spade, and Hervé Léger.[11]

Key processes. The company keeps its advertising costs in check by making smart use of its website and social media. Photographs are a huge part of RTR's popularity, with at least 10 percent of customers posting them on its Facebook page or website.[12] As an incentive for posting, other customers can "like" your photos, and getting hundreds of "likes" from people across the country can be exciting.

Logistics is another key process with thousands of units of inventory being sent out, over and over. To manage their inventory of designer dresses, and again control costs, all dresses are stored, serviced, and shipped from one large warehouse in New York City. Inventory management has been outsourced to Slate NYC, a full-service dry cleaner, which helps keeps the dresses looking and feeling newer for longer. Dresses are retired after 8–15 wears.[13]

Originally, the firm outsourced its website development, but management recently added a full-time technology leader to the leadership team.[14] The website is always being updated to help customers find dresses that would look good on them. Members can upload their measurements to help assess fit, and they can also chat with stylists or even other site users about what the clothes feel like, what cuts and sizes would be best for their body types, and, ultimately, what they might look like in a beautiful couture outfit.

Data are mined to determine how often the dresses get rented, and which dresses are popular with different age groups and in different geographic areas. For instance, dresses from designers such as Lela Rose, Milly, and Shoshanna, which are more feminine and conservative, tend to be more popular in the South while boho-chic styles tend to be more popular on the West Coast.[15]

Profit formula. Information about the firm's profit formulation is difficult to find, but the company purchases its dresses at wholesale and maintains an inventory of 25,000 current and recent-season dresses that mostly cost between $400 and $2,000 at retail. Generally, rentals are priced in the neighborhood of 10 percent of the retail price.[16] According to Reuters, the company had a revenue of about $6 million in 2010 and it increased to $20 million in 2011.[17] Quora reports that the company has been profitable since March of 2011.

Customer value proposition. The value proposition for this company is clear. The company offers young women a chance to wear beautiful clothing at a very reasonable cost, and they make it easy to do it. You can even be sure that your dress will fit because you get two sizes for the price of one. When you're done, you stick it in the envelope and mail it back.

The company also offers a subscription to make reserving a dress even easier. For a 1- or 3-month period, subscription members can pick up as many dresses as they want without worrying about the incremental cost. They also don't have to worry about whether the dress they're reserving is a $75 Diane von Furstenberg or a $200 Herve Leger—they're all covered under the flat subscription fee.[18]

RTR keeps its costs low with careful inventory management and the use of only one large facility. It constantly surveys customer purchasing behavior to enhance the selection of dresses, designers, and sizes available.

How Does It Create Value for Customers?

Like the TOMS' model, customers found value in this value proposition right out of the box. The model is powerful, because it provides value at several different levels of customer goals and aspirations. How does it do it?

First, the company is obviously solving a problem for the customer, and that is, what to wear on that special event, or what to wear when you want to feel beautiful. In addition, at a functional level, RTR obviously reduces the costs associated with finding the right thing to wear for an event. You don't have to drive from store to store searching for the right dress, you don't have to spend hundreds of dollars to buy it, you don't even have to get it dry-cleaned after you wear it—you just stick it in the mail and its gone. As for benefits, the fun of choosing the dress, the anticipation associated with wearing it, and the memories afterward are all rated highly by customers. In fact, a customer survey showed that members rated the emotional connection to the rental experience as more important than functional benefits such as getting the garment for 8 days, or getting an extra size for free.[19]

The strength of this emotional connection indicates that RTR is satisfying customer's long-term goals and aspirations and appealing to their sense of self. RTR provides value to women by helping them define who they are and establish how they want to be perceived.

Is the Model Sustainable?

Figure 7.2 shows RTR's adaptive business model. I use this to discuss changes and additions that are now being made to enhance sustainability.

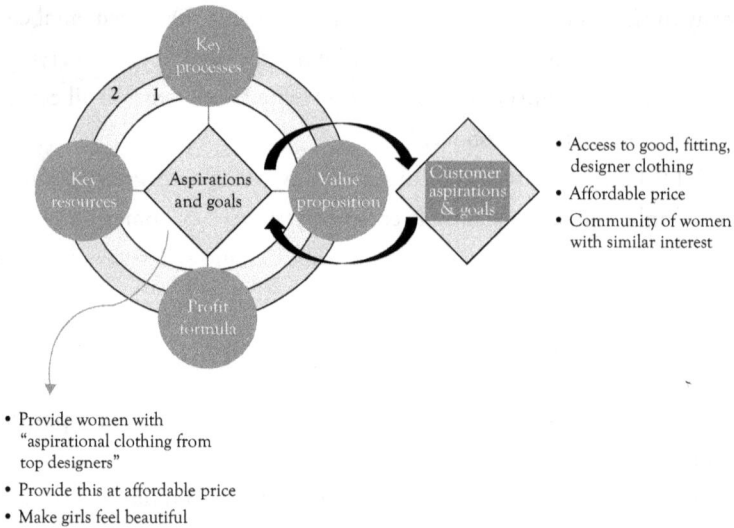

- Access to good, fitting, designer clothing
- Affordable price
- Community of women with similar interest

- Provide women with "aspirational clothing from top designers"
- Provide this at affordable price
- Make girls feel beautiful

Figure 7.2. Rent the Runway adaptive model.

Building and Leveraging Customer Relationships

Unlike Netflix, RTR irrefutably incorporates customers into its business model. The firm strives to build an ongoing relationship with young women, from high school prom days through college and beyond and to provide them with an introduction to Alice & Olivia, D&G, Missoni, Diane von Furstenberg, Trina Turk, and other designers, who will assist them on the way.[20] It places a heavy emphasis on marketing to college campuses and a few elite prep schools, which comprise about 25 percent of the company's business, and are a big source of its growth.[21]

A key process related to building customer relationships involves recruiting a network of approximately 150 "runway representatives" at 50 college campuses to promote RTR rentals before major campus events. Sororities are key targets. These student representatives hold fashion shows, build blogs and Facebook pages, and host rental parties in exchange for building their resumes and getting discounts on their own clothing rentals.[22] Some schools even award college credit for this activity.[23] This process of involving customers in sales activities is an excellent example of how a company can integrate the customer base into the business model. It has worked so well that RTR is planning a similar system for prep schools.

The company's Facebook pages also create opportunities for customers to discuss events they have attended and how they styled their particular outfit. Says Fleiss, "Natural dialogue is happening between our consumers."[24] Surprisingly, 15–20 percent of their users are men who want to rent a dress for their girlfriends.[25] By chatting with female customers online, they can get a better idea of what type of dress they should order. This idea of customers helping other customers choose styles is also an example of customers assisting with selling the RTR product.

Fleiss and Hyman also use RTR's social media sites as opportunities for learning from their customers. Both actively participate in RTR's social media efforts, hosting "style chats" on Twitter with consumers to get ideas and style tips. It was a customer who gave them the idea to prealter all their gowns in three lengths, and the company implemented it immediately.[26] They also take part in "style counsels," where they post dresses on RTR's Facebook page after designer runway shows and ask customers to vote on which ones they want purchased for the website. According to Jenny Fleiss, "Essentially, we're incorporating them into our buying process, in which their feedback is instrumental in choosing what products we decide to offer on our site."[27]

Finally, the company recently hired Maxymiser, a firm that specializes in multivariate testing, personalization, and optimization solutions to conduct comprehensive website testing. "Rent the Runway is truly an innovative and progressive online business," said Mark Simpson, founder and president of Maxymiser. "Not only will we help them deliver a better online customer experience, but we can also help them better understand who their customer is based on certain shopping criteria like previous searches, rentals, time of day, demographics, geography, and more. At the end of the day, when you know your customers better, you're able to serve your customers better. It's as simple as that."[28]

Jennifer Hyman agrees that the use of personalization, big data, and social networking is making it easier to find what you want, but in the end, she contends, it's the human touch and the interaction between shoppers that separates RTR.[29]

How the RTR Rental Model
Is Changing Industries

The essence of the RTR business model is the belief that the firm can change the way that women think about buying clothing—particularly for special events. Both leaders talk about the wisdom of investing in basics, like a little black dress that can be worn many times, while renting dresses for occasions, where one should never be seen with the same dress twice. In addition, they stretch the idea of a special event to include anything from formal dances, to first dates.

As I have said throughout this book, every now and then, a new business model comes along and transforms our old ways of doing things. Netflix did this in the DVD rental industry and as a result it forced Blockbuster and many other video rental stores out of business. The Netflix model may do it again in the retail clothing industry but for a different reason. Customers have been renting movies for years; Netflix just made it easier. But for most women, the idea of renting fashion ware is a new one. In the clothing industry, RTR is a leader in the promotion of collaborative consumption. *Collaborative consumption* is a type of business model in which shared goods or services are distributed via a market place to a community of users.[30]

According to Tomasz Tungez in the *MIT Entrepreneurial Review*, collaborative consumption reshapes markets by changing supply and demand economics. Using Zipcar as an example, he points out that these new market places shrink consumer retail demand since each shared car eliminates 5–20 cars from circulation.[31] Similarly, he says, a college textbook rented 10 times over its life will replace between 5 and 7 new copies.

Collaborative consumption also has potential to increase demand and the total market size by addressing new previously unaddressable segments.[32] Until RTR came along, for instance, women in Starkville, Mississippi or Stillwater, Oklahoma could not easily acquire designer gowns at affordable prices whenever needed.

In 2011, *Time Magazine* called collaborative consumption one of the 10 ideas that will change the world.[33] It is likely that the emergence of this model in many different industries may have been inspired by customers in their twenties and early thirties who have had a tougher time in the job market, and who carry high levels of college debt. According to a recent article in Bloomberg Businessweek, many members of this generation are insecure about the future and prefer to rent what they need when they need it in order to stay flexible.[34]

Like Zipcar, RTR's collaborative consumption model is a business to consumer version. More recently, peer-to-peer options are emerging. For example, women could share clothing with other women, and families share houses, sometimes free, sometimes for a fee. These models are very inexpensive to get off the ground because, instead of purchasing assets, you get them from the community, often in exchange for a revenue share of the transaction.[35]

With these trends converging, it is highly likely that the effects of collaborative consumption modeling are just getting started. As Botsman and Rogers state, it is a "socioeconomic groundswell" that will transform the way companies think about their value propositions—and the way people fulfill their needs.[36]

The Long-Term View for RTR

The future for RTR is certainly not assured, given the many changes that are now taking place as business models collide and erupt around them. Yet, they are doing many things to enhance their learning and adaptability.

First, the leadership team has proven that it listens. They are adept at using their business model as a learning tool and involving their growing customer base in the process. They use technology to study customer purchase patterns, they survey customers directly about features and benefits, they hold live chats on Twitter, they facilitate conversations on Facebook, and they connect customers with each other to converse about the products. Both on their websites and on college campuses, customers are selling their products to other customers!

The company is also experimenting with a new way to gain customer feedback by opening a small retail storefront in New York City, thereby changing the business model from online only. This shop allows women to try on clothes by different designers to understand which styles fit their body types, and work with stylists to gain new ideas and perspectives as they make their decisions.

Of course, the RTR leadership duo also has to pay close attention to the many types of new competitors that are emerging rapidly. For instance, Girl Meets Dress is a U.K. firm with a very similar model, and Ilus is a New York City retail store renting luxury dresses based on the original men's tux rental approach, which is a legitimate substitute for women who would prefer to try the clothes on.

RTR executives are aware of the ongoing industry evolution and are thinking strategically about the future. They have recently introduced bridal wear into their lineup and they are promoting dress and accessory rentals for all occasions surrounding the wedding, from the engagement party to the bridal shower and honeymoon. Their research shows that brides tend to buy an average of six dresses each for their weddings. They are hoping to change this behavior.

When asked about their future direction, they referred to the many different options that they may consider. "When we think about which product categories we should extend into or which demographics we should go after, or even which countries we should consider, it's all about kind of balancing that in a strategic and thoughtful way."[37]

Summary and Conclusions

This chapter has focused on the story of how two Harvard MBA students spotted an opportunity to create a new type of value for customers wanting to look beautiful at a special event. The team has built a business model that not only meets these needs, but also incorporates customers into their decision making and promotional processes. In addition, the RTR model has introduced a big change into the traditional retail clothing industry by teaching women to rent as opposed to buy certain types of clothing. This transformation is another threat to an industry that has already been under siege from a growing cadre of new online competitors.

In the next section, I talk about J.C. Penney, a grand old dame in the retail department store segment, and I look at its struggle to change gears and reshape its old business model.

CHAPTER 8

J.C. Penney's Big Experiment

In the past several chapters, I have used three different business model lenses to talk about how firms create, deliver, and capture value. I have also explained the logic that companies use in making decisions about their business models, and have talked about ways that new models can transform industry environments. In fact, a key theme across many of these stories is that new business models are emerging more quickly than ever before and that old models are being undermined as a result.

A key takeaway is that regardless of how great your business model is, it won't work forever. A recent blog by Ron Ashkenas was called "Kill your business model before it kills you."[1] In it, he pointed out that Kodak hung on to its film business long after the introduction of digital media and AOL knew that dial-up subscriptions were declining far before it took action. The moral was that many firms put off business model change, even those that see the writing on the wall.

Changing your business model is difficult because it requires changes in resources, processes, norms, and policies all across your organization. It may also require changing the type of employees you hire. And all of these changes must be made in a holistic fashion, so that they are consistent and mutually reinforcing. These are comprehensive changes at a deep level. And yet, to succeed in the long run, you must be ready and willing to take your company in new directions when the situation calls for it.

Keeping a business model viable is a continuing task.[2] A model that is initially sound should withstand economic ups and downs but can become dysfunctional if major discontinuities occur.[3] In fact, it is possible to envision a business model life cycle in which new models are introduced, refined, adapted, revised, reformulated, and, eventually, rejected. When external changes undermine a model, it often cannot be recalibrated; a new model must be constructed.[4]

Johnson, Christensen, and Kagerman describe five strategic circumstances that often require business model change.[5]

1. **To serve new or emerging markets.** If you identify a group of customers who have been shut out of a market, this may be a worthwhile opportunity for developing a new model. Sometimes customers have missed out because of money, but other times, it may be due to lack of education or even lack of access. Rent the Runway actually identified an underserved market of women who did not have access to designer dresses easily or affordably.

2. **To capitalize on new technology.** If you have the opportunity to leverage a new technology by finding a way to bring it to new customers, then a new business model may be warranted. Netflix saw streaming as a new technology and changed its business model to make it work. Unfortunately, the firm forgot to consider its customers.

3. **To bring a job-to-be-done focus where none exists.** Bomgar found a way to solve a major problem for customers who didn't realize it could be solved, by allowing computer technicians to tap into their customers' computers from a distance. This was an unmet need and the company stepped in to fill the gap.

4. **To fend off low-end disrupters.** Netflix also saw the need to change because companies such as Hulu, who had a much less expensive infrastructure by focusing only on streaming, were entering the movie rental market.

5. **To respond to a shifting basis of competition.** Over time, many different developments and forces can converge to change the way you compete in an industry. This is happening in many industries today but one that has been hit particularly hard is the retail industry. As we have seen in past chapters, new channels have opened up, as well as many new forms of competitors.

The next section explores how one competitor, J.C. Penney, is attempting to respond to this confluence of changes by transforming its business model.

J.C. Penney Background

J.C. Penney was originally founded in 1902 by James Cash Penney in Kemmerer, Wyoming, where it sold clothing to frontier miners, farmers, and their families.[6] Originally, Penney called his store the Golden Rule because he believed in treating others the way he himself would want to be treated. From this small beginning, the firm rose to become the second largest retail chain in the world, following Sears. At its height, there were 2,053 Penney stores across the country, down to about 1,100 in 2012.

A quote from a 1908 advertisement gives a glimpse of the firm's original customer value proposition:

> We are here to stay; we like the country—its people; we believe in selling you good dependable goods on a Small Margin of Profit Only. We will supply you with durable and comfortable wearing apparel cheaper than ever before. You will get BIG VALUES for your money at this store. Let competition say what she will. A comparison of values is all we ask... Our aim is to sell you Reliable, Staple, Dependable Merchandise at a less price than any other house in the country.[7]

As this quote shows, J.C. Penney got its start by providing its customers with quality clothing at lower prices than the competition, and it kept this same basic value proposition for a hundred years. The fact that this company is 110 years old suggests that it has been highly effective at adapting and transforming its business model over time as the industry evolved and as competition grew.

Today, J.C. Penney is categorized as a department store chain, meaning that it offers an array of goods, usually with different brands, organized into departments. Generally, they not only emphasize apparel and shoes, but also have departments that carry anything from jewelry and makeup to home furnishing and kitchen items. Appliances and other hard goods such as hardware are less likely to be included.

The department store business is under increasing pressure these days, which I explore in the next section.

The Rise (and Fall) of Department Stores
and J.C. Penney in Particular

When they emerged in the late 1800s, department stores had everything from restaurants and tea rooms, to art galleries, live music, and fashion shows.[8] The original competitors, such as Macy's and Lord & Taylor (New York), Marshall Field (Chicago), and Jordan Marsh (Boston), were located in cities around the country and were dubbed palaces of consumption.[9] For most of the 20th century, they reigned as centers of commerce and hubs of social activity.[10] They were where people shopped for everything from clothing and jewelry, to electronics, home goods, and appliances. According to Lewis:

> During this period, much of the U.S. population resided in rural areas, far from these "palaces." These original department stores offered such an overwhelming and compelling experience that those rural families would tear themselves away from the Sears catalog, the Internet equivalent of the time, to travel for hours to these beautiful and exciting stores and to spend the entire day enjoying and probably spending more, just for the experience.[11]

Part of the allure of these early department stores was their atmosphere and decor, making the shopping experience a form of entertainment. At one time, these stores were the fashion monitors of the day and led the way with new trends in retailing. They were the first to provide consumer credit and to create mass-produced clothing, and they became the home for national fashion designers.[12]

J.C. Penney did not start out as one of these palaces of consumption. As noted earlier, it was founded in the rural west, as a clothing store targeted at working families, and it initially morphed into a mass merchant, carrying home appliances, hardware, auto supplies and service, and the like along with its clothing and home goods. This format helped it to expand quickly across the country, locating in large and small cities alike, but mostly attaching itself to suburban malls. It was not until the 1980s that Penney's actually repositioned itself as a department store, eliminating many of the hard goods based on the premise that customers don't go to malls to buy washing machines.

Ironically, it was at about that same time that Walmart and a new cadre of mass merchants began stealing customers away from department stores with their everyday low prices and wide assortment of merchandise. Target added to the competitive mix by enhancing the selection and shopping experience in a mass merchant setting. T.J. Maxx and Ross Stores also leaped into the fray with their discount "department" store models, offering similar goods to department stores, but with less ambiance and lower prices. A wide array of specialty stores began to appear, focusing on the latest fashions for the growing teen and student market. Off-price and outlet stores popped up all around the country. With so many new stores opening up, the sheer amount of retail space in the United States skyrocketed in the last part of the 20th century. And then in the 2000s the Internet exploded.

The growth of online stores, such as Amazon.com, and Zappos now poses a major threat to the department store industry. Not only have these web-based competitors stolen sales from traditional stores, but they have also changed the way consumers shop. One analyst pointed out that the growth of online sales is causing retail stores to change into mini-distribution centers for the Internet. This trend is increased as retailers put in place "buy online, pick up in store" programs such as Toys 'R Us has done.[13]

The growth of so many new options, combined with the poor economy over much of the past few years has continued to wreak havoc with traditional department stores. In response, the department store segment has consolidated, with industry leaders buying weaker chains, leaving only about 20 companies operating approximately 3,500 stores with combined annual revenues of some $60 billion. Along with J.C. Penney, major players include Sears, Macy's, Neiman Marcus, Nordstroms, Saks, and Dillard's. Many of the stores have been striving to draw in customers by using heavy discounting techniques. Macy's is a good example of a department store that runs frequent promotions, but J.C. Penney's may have been the leader with over 590 unique promotions in 2011.

That year, Penney's sales fell about 2.8% to $17.3 billion from the previous year. For the first time, its revenues were surpassed by Kohl's[14] (also a heavy discounter), which rang up 18.8 billion in sales. Macy's sales for that period exceeded 26.5 billion. As a comparison, Walmart rang up over $446 billion in sales in the same period, almost as much as the entire department store segment.[15]

In 2012, Penney's also lagged behind Macy's and Kohl's in terms of both gross margins and operating margins. Its sales per square foot of $132 was only half that of Kohl's and about 30% below Macy's.[16]

From this brief description, several points deserve attention. First, J.C. Penney evolved from a little store in Wyoming to the second largest retail chain in the nation. Along the way, it first transformed itself from an apparel store to a mass merchant to a department store. Yet, today, the entire department store industry is in decline and is facing questions about its relevance to customers. Moreover, Penney's has fallen behind other major players. Yet, while it's $17 billion in sales in 2011 was far less than Walmart, it was far more than Rent the Runway. And with over 1100 retail locations across the country, and with its strong history, the firm would seem to have the resources to support a turnaround.

J.C. Penney's Business Model Transformation

In 2011, Ron Johnson, from Apple, was hired to turn the company around. Johnson, known both for designing Apple's beautiful retail stores, and for helping to establish Target's aura of cheap chic, announced that he would treat the chain "like a start-up company"[17] by reformulating its business model and reinventing the department store. To assist him in revamping the stores, he installed Michael Francis, another former Target executive, as J.C. Penney's brand president.

The first question to ask about the change at J.C. Penney's is whether this is truly a business model change versus a strategic repositioning. If we consider only the most basic elements of its business model, or the foundation, we might say that not much has changed. The company is still a department store with a chain of retail outlets, a broad array of goods, and supporting online sales. However, if we consider the differentiated business model lens shown in Figure 8.1, we can see that Johnson's revision is addressing every element in the circle, a sign that true business model remodeling is occurring.

Leadership and vision. Fresh from his leadership stint at Apple, Johnson attributes that company's success to its innovative retail stores,

- More stores being leased
- Cutback in mailings, coupons, and promotions
- Special discounts
- New approach to advertising
- Move to mobile checkout devices

- Remodeling hundreds of stores
- "70 new stores"
- Change from 18 to 13 supply chain locations
- Reduction in number of employees
- Change to more designer brands
- New "jcp logo"

- Fashion brands at everyday fair prices
- Providing value in the "experience"

Key processes

Key resources

Johnson's aspirations & goals

Value proposition

Profit formula

2   1

- Lowering cost structure
- Creating platform for growth
- New targeted expense reduction
- New sales objectives
- Cost cuts

- Johnson's experience at Apple
- Make Americans live and look better everyday
- Reinventing what it means to be a department store

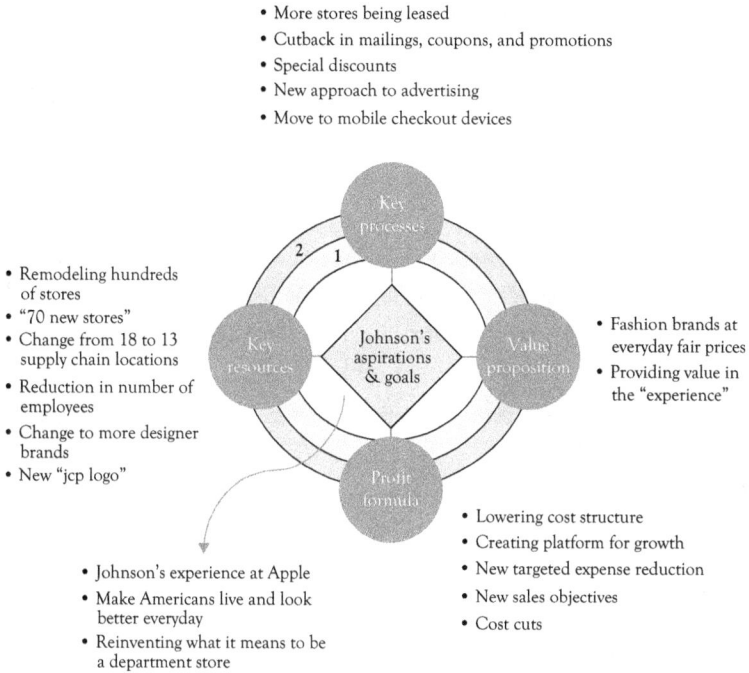

Figure 8.1. Changes to J.C. Penney's differentiated business model.

which succeeded when other computer retailers such as Gateway were failing. "When you begin with a vision of enriching lives vs. moving boxes, magical things happen," he says.[18] His vision for the new J.C. Penney is just as compelling. He wants to help Americans live and look better every day, and he wants to make J.C. Penney their favorite store.[19] How? According to Johnson, "We think the promotional model is going away. We're going to create a new category. We're going to call it: the specialty department store. It's going to be profound," he says.[20]

As opposed to trying to change J.C. Penney from a department store to another type of retailer, Johnson is trying to reinvent what it means to be a retail department store. And ironically, his changes sound a lot like the original department store business model, from the 1800s, when department stores were like self-contained mini-malls, with fashion shows, and tea shops and live music. With his proposed store-within-a-store concept, Johnson seems to be bringing the notion back to life.

Key resources. The company is completely remodeling hundreds of stores, using the store-within-a-store concept. Each grouping is based on one brand-specific item or a collection of similar items. Widened aisles will lead to a central location called The Square, where Wi-Fi and refreshments will keep customers in the store.[21] The 700 or so smaller stores in the chain are getting some changes as well including a new store layout built on small clusters. If all goes as planned, the company will open 70 new stores by 2014.

The company's distribution system has also been streamlined from 18 supply chain locations to 13. The firm also operates six logistics hubs that serve as the entry point for direct imported goods. Although these will not change, two call centers have been closed. In addition, over 600 employees were laid off at the company's Plano, TX headquarters, and employees have been cut from the payroll at stores all across the country. Commissions for its sales staff were also eliminated.

Traditional Penney brands, such as St. John's Bay and Ralph Lauren, have been dropped while new designer names such as Vivienne Tam and Betsey Johnson have been added. The plan is to increase sales of national brands to 75 percent versus the former 45 percent.[22] Finally, the J.C. Penney store brand has been replaced by a new "jcp" logo.

Key processes. In the new jcp stores, only some of the store groupings will be run in-house, while a greater percentage will be leased to companies such as Sephora.

Mailings, coupons, and promotions have been dramatically cut back and replaced with an everyday, fair-and-square pricing approach in which products are said to be priced at a level 40 percent lower than the former presale regular prices. Special discounts are offered on Fridays and monthly discounts are in place for slow-moving items. This change from a discounting to a fair price approach also allowed the firm to lower its advertising budget by about $300 million a year.

To introduce its new approach, the company hired Ellen deGeneris as its spokesperson. In another new approach to advertising, it included images representing gay and lesbian parents in its mothers and fathers day promotional materials. The idea was to promote all kinds of American families.

The company also announced plans to replace its old-fashioned cash registers with mobile checkout devices similar to those used in Apple stores. jcp is also introducing self-checkout kiosks. It is even considering the total elimination of cash purchases in the near future. jcp will also replace the conventional bar-code tags with Radio-Frequency Identification (RFID) tags that will enable customers to check out without physically scanning individual items.[23]

Profit margin. By simplifying J.C. Penney's operations, significantly lowering the company's cost structure and creating a platform for growth, the company seeks improved profitability in 2012 and beyond.[24] Specifically, a targeted expense reduction of $900 million was announced in January 2012 and a sales objective of at least of $177 per square foot has been set for 2015. Although cost cuts to date have been substantial, they have not yet paid off, particularly because Johnson has undertaken to transform so many stores at one time, an expensive proposition.

Customer value proposition. On the surface, the new value proposition is based on offering fashion brands at everyday fair prices in an exciting retail environment framed by a store within a store concept. Restating this, instead of providing a spot where customers can treasure hunt, or look for bargains, jcp will provide a spot where shoppers will find value in the experience, where they can get free haircuts, and sip coffee, and use Wi-Fi, while not having to worry about coupons or digging through sales racks.

Since this is a total revision of the former "popular brands at a discount" proposition, the jury is still out concerning whether customers will perceive this proposition as something of value. In other words, in attempting to transform J.C. Penney's business model in so radical a way, Johnson is actually conducting an experiment worth billions of dollars to shareholders. So the big question is: Will it work?

In May 2012, only 6 months into the change, it was announced that company sales were down 20 percent. The next day, the company experienced the largest percentage decline in stock price since 1929. Francis left a month later, and Johnson took over the marketing responsibilities along with his role as CEO.[25]

Johnson likened the turnaround efforts to a marathon. "We said this would be a very tough year. I don't think that got through," Johnson says.[26] In the meantime, critics have questioned whether Johnson fully understands the J.C. Penney customer.[27]

What About the Customers?

The value exchange agreement between the new J.C. Penney's and its old customers as shown in Figure 8.2.

Johnson's vision, shown on the left, fits with his past experience at Apple and Target, and his knowledge of younger, style-conscious consumers. Apple set out to change the world, and it did, so why shouldn't J.C. Penney change the way people shop? If Johnson's changes are successful, the J.C. Penney stores will be transformed into lifestyle stores that will appeal to a younger customer who lives in a different world than the traditional J.C. Penney customer.[28]

On the right side of the model, we have J.C. Penney's core customer base consisting of older, price-conscious shoppers drawn to the company's frequent promotions and deep discounts. They have complained loudly about Johnson's transformations. Like Netflix, J.C. Penney's appears to have abandoned its customer base in search of new customers.

The most frequent customer complaints concern jcp's new fair-and-square pricing scheme. As some critics noted, the "price value" proposition made to shoppers was very complex.[29] Some merchandise was labeled as "everyday value." Other merchandise was discounted only on first and third Fridays, a policy that was changed to every Friday after only a few months. Coupons and promotions were eliminated despite the fact that they had driven consumers into their stores for years. As a result, many customers have abandoned Penney's to shop in stores such as Belk, Kohl's, and Macy's, all of which are promotionally driven, running sales on a regular basis, the same strategy that J.C. Penney used to employ.[30]

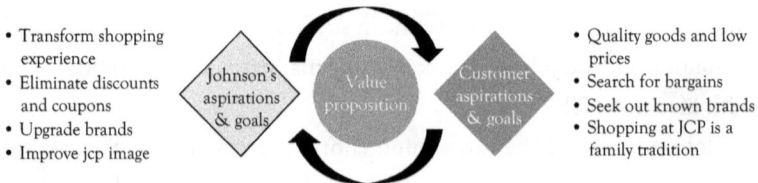

- Transform shopping experience
- Eliminate discounts and coupons
- Upgrade brands
- Improve jcp image

Johnson's aspirations & goals — Value proposition — Customer aspirations & goals

- Quality goods and low prices
- Search for bargains
- Seek out known brands
- Shopping at JCP is a family tradition

Figure 8.2. J.C. Penney's value exchange agreement out of whack.

Many customers have also complained about the change in the store's brands and product lines. The traditional J.C. Penney brands have been replaced with new "fashion" brands. Customer comments in online discussion boards repeatedly lamented the loss of valued brands and products, such as Cabin Creek blouses for women, and St. John's Bay trousers for men.

Another change that some customers didn't like related to some of jcp's new advertisements. As one former Penney patron said to me:

> "I didn't mind seeing Ellen DeGeneres in the commercials because she is a highly talented, and very funny woman. And she wasn't promoting her lifestyle so I could ignore it. These other ads with gay couples were a different story. I haven't been back to Penney's since. And that's sad because we've always been a Penney's family. My grandmother shopped there and so did my mother."

Whether you agree with this philosophy or not (and I don't), it is a fact that many of Penney's stores are located in conservative, rural communities. Taken together with the elimination of discounts, and the shift in brands, these messages seemed to suggest that the new jcp value proposition is actually aimed at a new customer base. As one analyst says, the entire marketing mix seems to be out of sync with the jcp target audience. From the start, it appeared to be a strategy that came out of the mind of Johnson rather than jcp's customer base.[31]

Like Reed Hastings at Netflix, Johnson has clearly made decisions that violate the chain's value exchange agreements with members of its current customer base. According to brand consultant Bruce Dybvad, "Retailers pay a steep price when they break a sacred covenant. Leaders of tomorrow will be those who effectively manage transformational change with the participation of their customers and keep their promises."[32]

Evaluating the Changes in J.C. Penney's Model

Johnson, Christensen, and Kagerman pose several questions that can be used to see if a new model makes sense. We can apply these to the new J.C. Penney model.

1. **Does it contain a focused, compelling value proposition?** At this point, in thinking about the situation at Penney's, I would say no. It is not clear who the customers are or why they should come to the stores. It does not seem to address the current customers at all.

2. **Do all the pieces of the model work together to get the job done in the most efficient way possible?** When looking at the elements of Johnson's new model, there appear to be some inconsistencies. Cutting staffing levels in the stores, for instance, may not be compatible with upgrading the service experience. Dropping well-loved store brands to add fashion brands that other stores may be carrying may not lead to differentiation.

3. **Can you create a new model that is unfettered by the negative influences of your core business?** In this case, Johnson is revising the entire core business, while still working within the fundamental core department store format. One of the steps to making this huge change involved removing many of the old store managers and installing new ones. Although this sounds draconian, it may have been done to ensure that the changes would be supported at the store level.

4. **Will the new model disrupt competitors?** The question is, why will customers leave Macy's or Target or T.J. Maxx, or Amazon, to shop at Penney's? The answer at this point is not clear. Johnson hopes to do this by creating a department store model that entertains as well as provides stylish merchandise. This hearkens back to the original department store model from the 1800s, which was successful for years. Perhaps its time has come again.

Business Model Change Is Difficult

Johnson has showed both vision and courage as a leader in attempting to remake a great American company such as J.C. Penney's. Although the initial results have failed to live up to expectations, there is no reason to expect that the transformation of such a large company with such a long history can be accomplished in under 2 years. The real lesson here is not about any of the specific changes that Johnson has made or not made, but in the ideas that all leaders must consider when striving to revamp their business models.

1. **Business model change is like starting over—a new value proposition is a new hypothesis and must be tested.** The bottom line is that business model change is extremely difficult for any company. As with any start-up, a new business proposition is just a hypothesis and so it must be tested with real customers to find out whether it will be attractive or acceptable to them. Johnson's test was very risky because it included the entire enterprise. He has spent millions on transforming stores. A safer path is to experiment on a smaller scale, make changes incrementally, and refine and revise along the way. Yet when a firm is publicly owned, this path may not be possible.

2. **Business model change is fundamental change. Changes across the organization must be internally consistent and reinforcing.** Business model change not only involves new products and processes, but it also involves changing rules and norms, and putting new systems into place in a holistic way. While striving to upgrade the jcp stores' image and brands, Johnson also fired managers and personnel all across the system, eliminated commissions, and lowered pay. Will these cuts allow him to provide the level of customer service needed to support his new store image?

3. **Business model changes require that clear messages be sent to customers.** jcp's new fair-and-square pricing policy sounds a lot like Walmart's everyday low prices. And its store layout borrows some ideas from Target. Its new advertisements are carrying signals about family as well as the changes in the store. How do we make sense of these messages? What do they say about the company's identity? Clarity is key in such a transformation.

4. **Business model change may mean starting something totally new.** No business model lasts forever. Company leaders should always be looking for new business opportunities to potentially replace the current model. If you only invest in refining today's business model you'll get locked into it. Testing, incubating, and investing in alternative models hedges against that possibility.[33] Perhaps Johnson could have experimented with an entirely new venture, milking jcp's revenues to build the new model.

5. **The value of the change can only be determined by the customers.**
Johnson wants to reeducate customers, change their approach to
shopping, and even make them look better. And while in theory it is
possible to "educate" consumers that coupons and sales don't matter, as well as try to change their view of family values, experience
shows that attempting to modify consumer beliefs and habits is a
daunting task.[34]

Obviously, if it is to succeed in creating value for its shareholders,
J.C. Penney must create value for its customers. This means its new value
proposition should be able to answer two fundamental questions: *Why
should J.C. Penney's current customers continue to shop at J.C. Penney?* and
Why should any of competitors' customers switch to J.C. Penney? If it is not
able to retain most of its customers and attract new ones, J.C. Penney
may fade into oblivion, along with Marshall Fields and Filene's and other
retailers that lost touch with their customers.[35]

Summary and Conclusion

The department store is in a precarious position these days, losing share
to many new types of retailers as well as online stores. J.C. Penney, at 110
years of age, is at the center of this industry and is attempting to revitalize
the industry with a new notion of customer experience and value. Interestingly, this vision looks a lot like the original palaces of consumption
that initially defined the department store experience. It is ironic that
Penney's with its working class roots is moving in this direction. It is perhaps inevitable that the transformation is proving to be difficult.

Yet, the real bottom line is that all business model change is difficult. Some of this difficulty can be avoided if you include customers in
conversations about the changes. In addition, conducting smaller tests as
opposed to testing the change on the entire enterprise could have provided him with inputs about which changes were most effective in creating customer value.

The next chapter summarizes the lessons about business modeling
that have been covered in this book and draws some conclusions to assist
you in reducing the inherent risks of putting a new model into place.

CHAPTER 9

Ten Key Ideas About Business Models

I wrote this book to provide you with a practical approach to understanding business models. To do this, I presented three business model lenses, the foundation, the differentiated, and the adaptive business models. These lenses can be used to guide your thinking about how to design an initial model to experiment with and to assist you in evaluating the strengths and weaknesses of your firm's present model. To find the material to use in writing this book, I studied academic articles, read popular books and articles, searched online, followed blogs, and talked to my friends in the business world. In this chapter, I describe 10 major themes that came into focus for me as I did this work.

1. **A business model is a conceptual tool.**
   It helps you think. It helps you evaluate. It helps you frame your stories. The business model lenses shown in this book can help you to consider ways to use the resources and processes at your disposal to create something of value for your customers while making money for yourself. They can be used as frameworks to lead your examination of your own company's processes and systems and help you to determine which combinations of activities are generating value, and which are not. They can make you think about how you are going to earn money and what outcomes are needed to meet your goals.

   Business model frameworks, like the lens models described here, are holistic models. That means they incorporate all of the elements needed to create, deliver, and capture value. You can use them to clarify the core logic behind your system.[1] Although there are examples of successful and unsuccessful business models, there is really no recipe for success. Every business model that I studied was shaped and molded, and tested, and remolded by its leaders, as they struggled to find the right combination of ingredients. Business modeling is not quite a science these days; in fact, it is definitely part art.[2]

The basic elements of business model design include key processes, key resources, a customer value proposition, and a profit formula explaining how it will make money.[3] In addition to these elements, the entrepreneur or leadership team is also a key part of the model, especially in start-ups, since the vision, values, and capabilities of these individuals are often essential to establishing the innovation or differentiation needed to form a unique model. As we saw in Chapter 4, Martin Jue's skills were clearly the key to his firm's ability to create a flow of innovative products while keeping costs low. And finally, established companies are advised to consider the customers and the customer relationships in their business models.

2. **A business model is also a system that is built into all the things you do.**

Once your business becomes an ongoing operation, once customers begin buying your products, and revenues begin flowing, your hypothesized business model will become built into your company. A business-model-in-use is a system that includes all the elements needed to create value for your customers and capture value for you. This system includes the way that you manufacture your products, the type of employees you hire, the brand that you choose, and the policies that you set, and so on.

Often this side of the business model is hidden or unclear to organizational participants. The reasons for many past decisions are forgotten. To revitalize your company and your relationship with your customers, you should take a hard look at everything you do and ask yourself how it contributes to building or capturing value. Chances are, you will find some things that no longer make sense. Perhaps they used to be valuable, but they're not now. Learning to make your business model explicit is often the first step to improvement or change.

3. **You can use different business model lenses at different times.**

Once you understand that a business model is a tool to help you plan, design, learn, and change, then it makes sense that you need to use the right tool for the job. As your company grows and becomes more complex, your model should too. The business model foundation lens focuses only on creating and capturing value. It is useful when you are generating your customer value proposition and determining how you will make money, but it doesn't consider how you will compete. The value proposition for TOMS' shoes promises customers to give a pair of shoes to a child for every pair sold. The vision is part of the value proposition.

The differentiated business model lens emphasizes a second layer of decisions to be made, those that relate to distinguishing your model from those of competitors. When you consider value through this lens, you must consider how your firm's deliverables will be superior to those provided by others. And you must consider how to avoid easy imitation. These considerations must be ongoing since new contenders are always entering the picture. Once TOMS' buy-one-give-one model became popular, competitors came out of the woodwork. BOBS' shoes were a direct imitation, but other companies such as Warby Parker Eyewear have copied the model in different industries. TOMS will have to continue to find ways to differentiate its company from imitators since this basic value proposition is easy to copy. At present, its strong brand name is a differentiator. To maintain that lead, it should continue to propagate its message, and involve itself with customers, as well as serve as an exemplar of the kind of good that companies can do for the world. I think that to maintain this role, it will have to be absolutely authentic in its efforts to be socially responsible, and it will have to be willing to redefine what that might mean. Giving away free shoes may not be enough in the long run.

The adaptive business model lens is a better business model for a firm such as TOMS because it includes the customers as actual parts of the model. TOMS' leadership, under Blake Mycoskie, is certainly having conversations about how to stay connected with their customers and how to keep them interested in their humanitarian activities. This is very different from the approaches used by Netflix and J.C. Penney, both of which made radical changes to its business model without consulting customers. In contrast, TOMS has already taken steps to engage its customers in changing the world by supporting discussions on college campuses and inviting volunteers to help deliver shoes.

Depending on where you are in the growth and evolution of your business, you can use any of these business model lenses as tools to help you design your business, or help you to study and understand the business model that you have in place right now.

4. **Always remember that the most important purpose of a business model is to solve problems for your customers.**
Your mission is to help your customers stop worrying and start getting on with their jobs, or their lives. You do this by solving a problem for them. Unless you can do this, and do it better than your competition, you won't be around very long. Joel Bomgar's technician experience allowed him to see exactly what it was that frustrated computer technicians and his computer science education prepared him to do something about it. His product, the Bomgar Box, was an immediate success. It offered a solution to a compelling problem faced by computer technicians and helped them to serve the customers.

It is less clear what job the new J.C. Penney's is trying to solve for its customers. When someone wants to shop, there are many different types of retail clothing stores, as well as more glamorous department stores, and many new online stores. If you don't like those, you can go to Walmart or Target. When it comes to shopping, there are tons of alternatives that serve the need. So, the question is, what problem is the new jcp really trying to solve? Some have speculated that the new model is designed to entertain customers or to make the shopping experience more pleasurable by simplifying the decisions to be made. It may be true that people are seeking a different shopping experience in this day and age.

With his experience and success in designing the Apple retail stores, Ron Johnson appears to have a deep understanding of today's retail customers. If his solution works, J.C. Penney may indeed be ahead of the curve.

5. **Sometimes your customers can solve problems for you.**

Many companies, including Rent the Runway (RTR), have already figured this out. Customers are more than just the endpoints in our processes. Customers can be resources. Customers can be innovators. They can even help to promote and sell your offerings.

A key reason why RTR is able to rent dresses online with no opportunity to try them on is because customers educate each other, on the website and on Facebook, about how certain dresses fit, or what body types they might suit.

Creating more ideas for customer collaboration can be an important source of innovation. The adaptive business model accomplishes this by forcing you to think about customers as a critical company resource. What they have to tell you is critical to ensuring that you can outdo the competition.

6. **Never forget that your customers are the ones who define what is valuable.**

An important thing to understand when crafting a business model, or when reconsidering your model in use, is that value is always defined through your customers' eyes. Every customer is motivated or driven to make a purchase by a complicated mix of needs and desires. These include higher level goals and aspirations, current concerns or jobs to be accomplished, and specific calculations about benefits versus costs. In general, if you can increase benefits and reduce costs while solving a problem or helping your customers fulfill their personal goals, you are on the right track.

When considering the actual product or service, customers weigh the costs and benefits. Benefits are everything that they like, including how the product functions, or tastes, or feels, or looks, as well as how it affects them emotionally, or physically, or cognitively. Costs are the sacrifices they make to use the product as well as the actual price that they pay.

Your customers will often make trade-offs among these costs and benefits when they choose to buy a product. Some will pay more to get better quality or other benefits, while others may choose to drive an hour to find a product at a cheaper price. Some customers may choose to limit their access to an online service in order to get it for free; others may be willing to pay for a stronger set of services.

Products that compete only on their specific ratios of benefits to costs are more like commodities. Customers can search widely online for such products, easily comparing features and prices. To overcome this and to differentiate your offering, you need to find a deliverable that is more personal, such as your relationship with the customer, or your brand image.

The TOMS example shows us how even shoes can become imbued with a higher purpose that appeals to consumers. These days, there are many potential customers out there who are looking for a way to contribute to making the world a better place. If you can solve a problem and help a person feel good about himself or herself, you have a better shot at making a sale. If you can reinforce a person's perception of herself as a good person, then your product benefits will resonate.

7. **Your deliverables include product, price, access, and the transaction/interaction.**
When you are trying to find just the right mix of features to appeal to your customers, don't forget that it's not just the product itself that matters. The deliverables that you bring to the market also include access, price, and the transaction or interaction that occurs when the product is purchased.

Sometimes access itself can be an important differentiator as it is with both Netflix and Rent the Runway. Netflix knocked Blockbuster out of the industry when it started shipping DVDs directly to customers' doors. Then the firm's management worried that streaming was an even easier means of access and that customers would prefer the option to download films immediately.

Price has always been important in the customer's value judgments, but now an array of new pricing mechanisms is emerging.

It's not just the amount that you charge, but also the way you go about doing it that matters. Some companies find that customers prefer paying small subscription fees over time, while others provide some services for free, and then charge for others. Some firms provide everything for free, and get their revenues from advertising. Some firms have a combination of revenue streams. Like anything else in your business model, finding the right pricing mechanism or pricing level may be a matter of experimentation.

The customer relationship begins with the actual transaction that occurs when your customer buys your product. This is called a transaction when it only involves taking a payment and ringing it up. It becomes an interaction when you communicate with the person who is paying for your product and do so in a way that makes that person feel good about doing business with you. Every transaction has potential to become an interaction. When that happens, your customers will not only feel positive about doing business with you, but will change their behaviors in order to do it again. Some customers will stay with a service provider who is slightly more expensive than others, simply because they enjoy the relationship.

8. **Never stop experimenting.**
Your customer value proposition is a hypothesis about what customers want. It must be tested on real customers. Experimentation is key, for both new companies and old ones trying to make a change.

Blake Mycoskie brought a duffle bag full of canvas shoes back from Argentina and convinced a popular L.A. shoe store to carry them. Jennifer Hyman and Jennifer Fleiss carried racks of luxury dresses to students at Harvard and Yale to see if they would rent them. In both cases, the products flew off the racks and they knew they were onto something. Ron Johnson, in contrast, bet his entire company in his transformation of J.C. Penney's business model. That is a risky path.

Experiments should be designed so that you can succeed even if your experiment fails. In other words, keep your experiments small if possible. Martin Jue used small, low-cost experiments as he built his ham radio business 40 years ago. Back then, he built a selectivity filter to enhance Morse code signals and ran an ad in a popular ham radio magazine to try and sell it. In his next test, he made the product more user-friendly, ran a bigger ad, and got a toll-free Watts line. Although these tests occurred over several years, he learned not only what his customers wanted right then, but also the importance of listening to them.

Today, the testing concept is the same but the speed has increased. What Martin did in three years can be accomplished in months given the use of Internet sales and online advertising. Access to customers is different. Investor expectations are also different. Yet, we need to remember, although it is beyond the scope of this book, that not all start-ups need to aim for the kind of growth demanded by venture capitalists. Martin Jue insists that purposeful testing, personal investments, and frugal spending, while they may take more time, can have very positive results because you end up owning your own company.

The idea of testing your business model is also very important, maybe even more important, for large established firms. When old business models lose effectiveness, as in the J.C. Penney case, experimentation is crucial. Yet, as Chesbrough points out, these experiments are often resisted since they may initially result in lower returns.[4] Witness the sudden resignation of the jcp executive after only 6 months of that firm's transformation. Experiments should be designed not only in a way that involves real customers paying real money, but also in a way that reduces the cost of negative results. J.C. Penney's systemwide experiment was a very expensive way to test customers' perceptions of the firm's new ideas about customer value and pricing in a retail setting.

The four tests that you should consider from your initial business model design until your firm is mature include feasibility (does it work?), viability (will they buy it?), sustainability (will it last?), and adaptability (can we change?).

9. **New business models are emerging every day.**
A major theme, cutting through all of the stories in this book, is that business models are changing. In fact, we are in the midst

of revolutionary change in many industries. Some of the trends identified in this book include the following:

- Vertically integrated firms are giving way to a more networked approach. While this has been going on for years, the speed of value chain destruction may be increasing as new "layer players" enter specialized niches. New start-ups can now more easily gain access to manufacturing and technology specialists across the globe. TOMS is an example of an orchestrator firm with far-flung operations.

- The influence of the Internet may have begun with Amazon, but it is still leading to the growth and eruption of new business models today. The ease through which the Internet, combined with mailing or streaming technologies, can get goods or services to people in remote locations is leading to models that provide new value to customers who could not get access in the past. This ranges from transportation to dresses. In addition, companies that got started online, such as Rent the Runway, are moving strategically to add typical brick-and-mortar facilities in a more blended approach.

- Customer cocreation is helping companies to rethink their understanding of value and to realize how much they can gain by considering customers as part of their business models.[5] Rent the Runway has done an excellent job, not only enrolling customers as members, but also enlisting the customers in the actual selling of their products.

- Collaborative consumption is increasingly invading new industry space with both new corporate models and peer-to-peer models emerging. A whole generation of customers may be changing their attitudes about buying goods versus renting them when needed.

- Some attention should be paid to the question of when to let a business model die. When is it time to reinvest the assets in entirely new venues and to create entirely new models?

As far as possible, every business model should be designed to evolve as managers and frontline workers learn new and better ways of doing things. Hamel calls this a dynamic business model.[6] In this book, I have advocated that a learning and review process should be built into every model as soon as a value exchange is established. Including the customers in the model is a good step toward this end. However, even more openness is essential for long-term sustainability and renewal.

10. **Always think strategically about your business model.**

David Teece argues that business models are more generic than business strategies. He says that you must couple strategy analysis with business model analysis in order to protect the competitive advantage you've gained from implementing your model.[7] I agree. As I pointed out in Chapter 1, a business model is not strategy, but it does reflect your strategy. You make strategic decisions about your business model when you decide which customers to target, and how to use your resources to generate an advantage over competitors. However, once you have established your model, it constrains your future strategic decisions. Netflix learned this after investing heavily in the infrastructure needed to deliver DVDs to customers' mailboxes. This worked very well until video streaming came available. Then it had to figure out how to compete with new entrants who had much less expensive resources and processes.

Strategic analysis is an essential step in designing a competitively sustainable business model.[8] Sustainability can only be achieved if you are providing superior value to your customers. When you think strategically about your business model, you are always focused on ways to stay ahead of the competition. You must also consider ways to stop them from replicating your model.

One key to avoiding replication is to ensure that the different parts of your business model are working together well as a system. Johnson, Christensen, and Kagerman say that it's not the individual resources and processes that make the difference but their relationships to one another.[9] You have to integrate your resources and process in unique ways. And your decisions about how to do this must meet the requirements laid out in your profit formula.

RTR is a good example of a business model in which the parts are not only consistent, but are mutually reinforcing. The high-quality dresses are purchased through partnerships with particular designers based on customer feedback. A partnership with a dry cleaner is used to manage the costs associated with storing and cleaning the dresses. The website is used not only to rent the dresses, but also to elicit communication from customers, who even provide photos showing how great you can look for your next event. Data from the website are continuously studied to evaluate which dresses are popular in which markets.

Strategic thinking is the most important role of the top management of any firm. And strategic thinking about your business model is critical to your current and future success. In this short book, I have provided three lenses that can help you to focus on all of the pieces of the model and to identify or clarify the logic that brings them together. You can use these lenses to design a new business model, or to study your current business model in order to come up with innovations and changes to serve your customers better than the competition.

A business model is a way of making your strategic choices explicit.[10] It provides you with a framework for deciding what to do and what not to do.[11] Ultimately, it can guide you toward making decisions that are unique and valuable, and that will lead you and your firm to sustainable competitive advantage.

APPENDIX A

Pricing Mechanisms

For the customer, the way the product is priced is a measure of its exchange value. If a customer believes that the product's benefits outweigh the sacrifices and the actual price, then he or she may purchase it. People traditionally think of pricing mechanisms such as charging a premium price for a differentiated product or service, charging a discounted price to attract new customers (short term or long term), or other mechanisms such as auctions, and so forth. However, the Internet and rapidly evolving technologies have brought with them a new wave of innovative pricing mechanisms.

For many entrepreneurs, these innovative pricing mechanisms have opened up many new profit opportunities, and they have created a more effective way to ensure that both parties in the transaction are getting what they want. They can communicate their product offering to a wider audience and at a more effective price than in the past.

It goes without saying that pricing is a huge part of the offer, and a poorly chosen pricing mechanism can hurt the offer. People often forget that the word "price" is really a synonym for many words including rent, tuition, fee, fare, rate, toll, premium, bribe, due, salary, commission, wage, and tax. To help entrepreneurs understand different ways they can price their products to avoid making a mistake, I provide a list of popular and innovative pricing mechanisms and include a brief explanation of how each one works:

- **Premium Pricing.** For differentiated products, or those that provide high value, you can charge a relatively higher price. Such high prices are charged for luxuries such as Mercedes automobiles, Ritz Carlton hotels, and Cunard Cruises as well as Godiva Chocolates and Grey Goose Vodka.
- **Penetration Pricing.** When new products are introduced to the market, some may choose initially to set the price

artificially low in order to gain market share. Once this is
achieved, the price is often increased. This can be a good idea
if the value of the product or service increases as more users
subscribe.

- **Economy Pricing.** Unlike penetration pricing, here the
long-term strategy is to keep costs down for the long term and
establish a no-frills low price. The supermarkets often offer
economy brands for soups, spaghetti, and so forth. In this
case, low price is often the key differentiator.

- **Product Line Pricing.** When you have a range of products
or services, your pricing may reflect the benefits of parts of
the range. For example, with car washes: a basic wash could
be $5, a wash and wax $6, and the whole package for $8.
Product line pricing seldom reflects the cost of making the
product since it delivers a range of prices that a consumer
perceives as being fair incrementally—over the range.

- **Freemium Pricing.** With a Freemium model, you give away
the basic services of your product for a limited period or for a
limited number of services, and then charge a fee after so many
weeks, or for the more sophisticated part of your services.
The catch here is that the functionality of your service or
product must be high enough such that a certain proportion
of your users will absolutely want to pay for the extension and
maintenance of the extras. In other words, your service must
provide benefits that are perceived as indispensable for certain
customers upon them experiencing it. Dropbox is my favorite
example. Two GB of storage are absolutely free, but once you
become addicted, they are not enough.

- **Dynamic Pricing.** In the article "Online Dynamic Pricing:
Efficiency, Equity and the Future of E-Commerce," the
authors claim that "dynamic pricing is merely a new version
of the age-old practice of price discrimination."[1] Price
discrimination is observable in many industries today, such
as discounts to senior citizens, charging high interest rates
to young buyers of automobiles, and different airline prices
depending on the time gap between purchasing a ticket and

the actual flight. However, dynamic pricing has taken on a new meaning with advancements in technology such as the Internet. Online companies are no longer tied to "menu prices" that affect many other institutions, and prices can be changed by simply updating a web page. Also, the Internet has made it possible to gather information on individual customers' preferences through cookies and other techniques that allow online retailers to make suggestions tailored to these preferences. Finally, these technologies have affected the way consumers shop, making it much easier for them to quickly compare prices against the prices of competing firms.

- **Advertising vs. Pricing.** Many firms allow advertising on their websites using different forms of pricing. One form is to charge companies a fee to advertise on a site for a predetermined period of time. For example, $1000 gets you 1 month of banner ads. Next, websites such as Google and Yahoo charge users to be a "sponsored ad" where a company wishing to advertise shows up first when someone searches for a certain category. Also, many websites, including Facebook, have a form of advertising called pay-per-click advertising where the person wishing to advertise buys a certain amount of "clicks." Finally, many advertisers are pushing for a pricing structure where the price for advertising reflects the effectiveness or results of using different ads. Because the revenues are generated by the advertising fees, customers may be given access to these sites for free. In some cases, customers can choose to use a site free with ads or they can pay to view the site with no advertisements.

- **Paywalls.** Magazines and newspapers are the most common users of this type of pricing. The Internet led many subscribers of traditional newspapers and magazines to cancel their subscriptions and start viewing content online. Websites and blogs such as the Huffington Post started offering similar content for free, leaving traditional newspapers and magazines struggling to keep up. Many newspapers started offering content online, but could not find a way to earn a profit because users were viewing the information for free. To solve this problem, the paywall was developed. Typically, companies utilizing a paywall allow users to view a small portion of their content for free (similar to a freemium), but charge users to get full access to the site. According to one article, more than 20 percent of newspapers will utilize paywalls "...by the end of 2012."[2]

- **Pay-per-use Pricing.** The most notable pay-per-use platform today is Apple's iTunes. Apple will let users of their program listen to a portion of a song for free, but charge them a fee to buy the full version of the song. Also, the online application market for smartphones is adapting this type of pricing, where users can often download a trial version of an application for free, but users must pay to access the entire application. Information technology in general seems to be moving in the direction of pay-per-use pricing. An online article claims, "Going forward, [Information technology] will be a service paid for on a usage basis rather than an asset that you buy and put inside your corporation."[3]

- **Yield Management Pricing.** This type of pricing is typically pursued by companies who are constrained by capacity or timing who wish to maximize their revenues. For example, hotel and airline companies often struggle to fill rooms or seats during certain parts of the year, and simply do not have enough rooms or seats during peak times of the year. This pricing mechanism ensures that revenues are maximized during both cycles, by lowering prices during slow times to stimulate demand and fill rooms or seats, and raising prices (often significantly) during peak times to optimize their revenues.

- **Fixed Cost Pricing (Sticky, menu).** Although many firms seem to be moving away from this type of pricing, it is still important to note. Under this type of pricing, prices are often fixed at a given level for different reasons. First, customers often get used to prices charged by a firm and will respond negatively to changes in price. Consumers get used to a price and firms find it hard to increase the price, even if economic theory suggests they should. Next, it is often unreasonable for a firm to change the price of a good or service because of the associated costs of doing so. That is, a firm will incur costs of printing new menus, and so forth, which makes prices sticky in the short run.

- **Auctions (Dutch, English, Sealed Bid, Second-Price).** Auctions are one of the oldest and most common pricing mechanisms. Most people, however, do not realize there are multiple types of auctions. Each one will be briefly discussed.
  - **English.** Under this type of auction, an auctioneer begins the bidding (often times at a predetermined reserved price that must be met) and participants bid on the product. The auctioneer continues to increase the bid price until no one else is willing to bid on the product, at which time the bidder with the highest price buys the product.
  - **Dutch.** This type of auction begins with the auctioneer starting out at a price that is higher than the product is expected to sell for, then lowering the price in increments until a bidder agrees to buy. This type of auction usually takes very little time.
  - **Sealed Bid.** This type of auction involves bidders putting in a one-time bid in a sealed envelope. The bids are then opened, and the highest bidder wins the bid.
  - **Second-Price Sealed Bid.** Much like a sealed bid auction, the winner is the one with the highest bid. However, they pay the price offered by the second highest bidder. This form of auction is fairly uncommon.
- **Reverse Auction.** This form of pricing typically occurs when a buyer intends on purchasing a large amount of something in the future. The buyer announces a plan to make a purchase at some specific point in the future (6 months is typical), and the competing firms put together their best bid, which they place on the specified date. The end result is that the buyer typically receives a huge price discount as a result of the bidding, often at the expense of the bidder. This type of

pricing can put huge pressures on suppliers and small firms, who are afraid they will bid too low and not maximize their profits on the sale, or overbid and lose to a competing firm.

- **Negotiation.** Everyone at some point takes part in a negotiation. While more than just prices can be negotiated, this form of pricing involves both sides (the buyer and the seller) trying to convince the other to either raise or lower the price. Websites, such as Craigslist, bring the art of negotiation into the Internet age. Craigslist allows for users to post an online classified ad for products and services, which often include a price that the seller is looking to receive. Alternatively, buyers can also post ads indicating that they are looking to purchase something. Craigslist does not take part in the actual exchange, however, and the two parties involved in the exchange often negotiate over the asked price from the classified.

- **Cost-Plus Pricing.** With this form of pricing, a firm determines the total cost of producing a product or service, and then marks the price up in order to achieve a certain profit margin. For example, if the total cost to produce a beer is $1, a firm can price the product at $1 plus an extra 20 percent (for a total of $1.20) if they wish to earn a profit of 20 percent per unit.

- **Target Return Pricing.** This type of pricing helps investors determine what price they should charge in order to recoup their investment (plus an additional amount if they desire). For instance, if a group of investors wishes to recoup their investment of $100,000 in a beer company plus an additional 20 percent, and 100,000 units of beer are expected to be sold over the next year, then at the price of $1.20 per unit the investors can meet their target return.

- **Breakeven Pricing.** Similar to target return pricing, but instead of pricing at a point where the firm will earn a certain target return, the firm will set the price at a level that will help the firm break even. In the beer example, if 100,000 units are expected to be sold, price the product at $1.

- **Value-Based Pricing.** Pricing a product or service based on the value that a user of the product or service will get out of it. For example, installing solar panels on one's roof will save them an average of $20,000 over 5 years. Selling the product for $1000 would be of great value to the consumer, and charging an even higher price would most likely be acceptable. However, the person purchasing the product must perceive that a product will provide a certain amount of value (whether it will or not) for this to work.
- **Going Rate Pricing.** Simply charge the amount that other firms are charging for a similar product. For example, if a firm sells coffee in a small town, this firm will simply price their coffee at the same price as similar firms in the area.
- **Captive Product Pricing.** This form of pricing involves a firm selling you something at a steep discount in order to captivate you into purchasing something in the future. For example, Dell and other computer manufacturers will practically give you a printer with the purchase of a computer. They do this because they know that you will have to buy specifically designed ink cartridges for the printer at a steep markup in the future from them, making it very easy for them to recoup their investment.
- **Promotional Pricing.**
  - ○ **Loss-Leader Pricing.** Similar to penetration pricing. This usually occurs when a retailer sells a particular product at a loss in order to get people into the store. Although the store may lose money on one item, customers will hopefully buy more.
  - ○ **Special Event Pricing.** This form of pricing occurs when a firm offers a discount (or sometimes charges a premium) for a special occasion. For example, a baseball team might give a discount to veterans on Veterans Day.
  - ○ **Cash Rebates.** This occurs when a firm offers the buyer of a product a small reimbursement for purchasing the product. They often do so knowing that few consumers will actually go through the trouble of redeeming the reimbursement.

- ◦ **Coupons.** A form of advertising in which a consumer receives a discount for presenting a coupon that assures a discount for the product or service.
- ◦ **Warranties.** To convince consumers that a product or service will meet their expectations, companies often offer warranties that promise a refund to a defunct or unfulfilled product or service. Often companies will charge the buyer of a product for a warranty.
- **Channel Pricing.** This is best illustrated through an example. Consider how much you typically pay for a softdrink. It is likely that there is a discrepancy between the price you pay at the grocery store, a vending machine, or a restaurant. This discrepancy can often be very large. For example, a beer at an NFL football game can be upwards of $9.
- **Penalties.** This form of pricing is usually in addition to another form of pricing. It punishes customers for not holding up their end of the deal. For example, cell phone companies will often charge a penalty for going over your predetermined amount of minutes or data. Also, phone companies will charge you for canceling your contract. Banks often charge penalties for going over your limit in the form of overdraft fees.
- **Framing.**
  - ◦ **Pennies a day.** This type of pricing strategy involves putting the price of your product or service into a daily increment. For example, nonprofit organizations often use this strategy to convince people to donate to their cause. Asking for $50 dollars a year to support a child that the person making the donation most likely will never see sounds like a lot, but when these organizations say that you can feed a child for only ten cents a day, it seems reasonable to many people.
  - ◦ **Reverse Strategy.** By contrast, many nonprofits use the opposite of the pennies-a-day strategy to convince people not to do something. A good example of this is telling consumers how much they can save per year by not smoking.

○ **Odd and Even Pricing.** Some merchants will price a product at 9.99 vs. 10.00 because they believe that customers will perceive it as significantly lower.

There are many more forms of pricing mechanisms, and with the advent of new technologies there will certainly be more to come, but this should give you some ideas about how to price your product or service.

APPENDIX B

Online Marketplaces

The Internet has brought with it a completely new way of doing business for many entrepreneurs as well as already established businesses. It is no longer necessary for a business to have a brick-and-mortar store, mail catalogue, or even a company website to get products to customers. For example, there are thousands of businesses that use Amazon, Ebay, Buy.com, Craigslist, or other online marketplaces to communicate and negotiate with customers. Before these online marketplaces existed, many entrepreneurs did not pursue potentially profitable ideas because of the difficulty of communicating a product offering and getting that product to the end customer. I would venture to say that a majority of people who read this book have purchased something through one of these marketplaces. To give you a better understanding of how many popular online marketplaces work, and how you can use these marketplaces, I have listed 20 online sites here. These are culled from an excellent list called the "28 Leading Online Marketplaces" from the website 100auctionsites.com.[1]

1. **Amazon Marketplace**—Amazon Marketplace is a fixed-price online market that allows sellers to offer their goods alongside Amazon's offerings. Buyers are able to purchase new or secondhand items sold directly by a third party through the Amazon Marketplace. Sellers are charged a small commission based on the sale price, a transaction fee, and a variable closing fee.

2. **Buy.com**—Buy.com offers buyers a wide variety of products and reasonable prices on books, toys, jewelry, electronics, pet supplies, and many other items. It charges sellers a commission ranging from 8 percent to

15 percent depending on the category and ensures good traffic for all items since it has become a popular online retailer.

3. **Etsy.com**—This market is for handmade and one of a kind objects including handmade jewelry, vintage clothing, fine artwork, and crafts of all kinds. Etsy serves its clients by giving them publicity and accessibility to customers looking for one of a kind goods.

4. **Half.ebay.com**—Half.ebay.com is a popular marketplace for buyers and sellers alike. The site offers a broad selection of books, music, games, and movies. It is especially popular with students who use it for getting discounts on textbooks. The site charges a small commission to sellers.

5. **Ecrater.com**—Ecrater.com is a free web store builder and free online marketplace. This website does not charge a commission on sales. Products are posted to Google Product Search for increased trafficking.

6. **ioffer.com**—ioffer.com is an online community that allows you to buy, sell, and trade by negotiating. Its ability to simulate real-life transactions makes it a useful and helpful site. The site offers over 35 million items to negotiate on. The site has no listing fees.

7. **Bonanzle.com**—Bonanzle.com is an online market that is similar to Ecrater and Etsy. Its slogan is "Find Everything but the Ordinary," and it offers products ranging from artwork to antiques, coins and paper money, dolls, pottery and glass, as well as other craft-oriented items. All of the items on Bonanzle.com are unique in some way. Sellers can benefit from Bonanzla's featured items, as well as the setup of their own online stores.

8. **Newegg Marketplace**—Newegg Marketplace is the marketplace associated with Newegg, an electronics retailer. This site receives millions of visitors each month and includes jewelry, sporting goods, pet supplies, fragrances, and other assorted categories of items.

9. **MadeItMyself.com**—This website lists handmade items rom birdbaths to sachets. The many categories of items change frequently and include many unique offerings.

10. **ArtFire.com**—This site focuses on handmade items from individual artists. The categories include handmade, design, supplies, vintage, fine art, and media. Within those categories are even more subcategories to help buyers find what they are looking for. The items vary in style, material, color, and craft.

11. **Rubylane.com**—This marketplace claims its "Ruby Lane Advantage" is based on quality, security, and excellent customer service. It includes items related to fine art, antiques, and collectibles as well as unique jewelry pieces.

12. **Tias.com**—Tias.com also offers antiques and collectibles on the web. Most of the site's sellers are authentic antiques dealers who run shops of their own, and use Tias as an additional outlet to reach over 200,000 customers a day.

13. **Goantiques.com**—Goantiques.com brings together antique retailers and collectors. Goantiques.com has over 1,000 dealers from 31 countries who contribute a wide array of products to its Virtual Warehouse.

14. **Blujay.com**—Blujay.com is another online marketplace that is free to use. The site uses PayPal and Google Checkout to handle its transactions, and also posts listings to Google's Product service, thereby increasing customer traffic.

15. **Cyberattic.com**—Cyberattic.com is a marketplace for both buyers and sellers of antiques, home decorating items, and collectibles. Categories include children's collectibles, home decorating, silver, glass, memorabilia, and ephemera.

16. **Trocadero.com**—The site focuses on buying and selling art, antiques, home décor, and other collectibles. It is known for offering rare paintings, estate jewelry, and other popular collectibles. Fees range from $45 to $70 dollars a month for sellers and provide an array of promotional services.

17. **Atomicmall.com**—Atomicmall.com is a marketplace with spaces dedicated to sellers and buyers, making it easy to use and navigate. Sellers can join for free and are charged a small commission on sales. Sellers are also able to import offsite auctions (from say, your eBay listing), and utilize Paypal, Google Check Out, and Amazon

payment methods. Buyers can chat with Sellers in real time, and use one cart for multiple stores.

18. **Collect.com**—This marketplace is aimed at different kinds of collectors. It has a variety of categories, such as automotive, ceramic and glass, furnishings and fine art, jewelry and timepieces, collectibles, numismatics, outdoors, guns and knives, comics, music and movies, sports, and toys.

19. **Wigix.com**—Wigix.com is an online marketplace for buyers and sellers interested in electronics. It promises that you will "never overpay again," and provides a live pricing history that details how much the previous buyer spent on the product you're viewing. The structured catalogue makes it easy to find specific products and the Premier Product Destination catalogue includes user manuals, videos, reviews, blogs, and more to help customers make decisions. There are minimal "final value" fees for items above $25.

20. **Pricegrabber.com**—Pricegrabber.com is a service that allows sellers to list and sell merchandise easily and conveniently whether or not they have their own websites, and provides safe transactions for buyers as well. If you mainly want to drive buyers to your own website, you can select the pay per click method of payment (where you pay each time someone clicks on your ad). If you don't have a website, you can choose to use the Pricegrabber site to manage your transactions and then you will pay a percentage of your revenues upon each actual purchase. Pricegrabber includes many different categories from computers to appliances and furniture. The site attracts over 26 million visitors each month.

Once again, this is by no means a comprehensive list, and the number of online marketplaces available will undoubtedly continue to grow. They will be more tailored to specific products or market segments, meaning that entrepreneurs will have to do their homework to select the right online marketplace to utilize. Also, it might not be a bad idea to spread a business out among a few different online marketplaces to make sure you are reaching everyone you wish to reach.

Notes

Chapter 1

1. Stähler (2012).
2. Stähler (2012).
3. Stähler (2012).
4. Teece (2010).
5. Zott and Amit (2008).
6. Teece (2007).
7. Magretta (2002).
8. Linder and Cantrell (2000).
9. Teece (2010), p. 179.
10. Morris, Schindehutte, and Allen (2005).
11. Morris, Schindehutte, and Allen (2005).
12. Priem (2007).
13. Teece (2010).
14. Teece (2010).
15. Porter (1996).
16. Gray (2008).
17. Casadesus-Masanell and Ricart (2011).
18. Shafer, Smith, and Linder (2005).
19. Shafer, Smith, and Linder (2005).
20. Teece (2010), p. 182.
21. Teece (2010), p. 189.
22. Holloway and Sebastiao (2010).
23. Holloway and Sebastiao (2010).
24. Johnson, Christensen, and Kagermann (2008).
25. Sarasvathy and Dew (2005).

Chapter 2

1. Handfield (2006).
2. Handfield (2006).
3. Magretta (2002).
4. Timmers (1998).
5. Rappa (2001).
6. Teece (2010), p. 174.
7. Wong (2011).
8. Linder and Cantrell (2000).

9. Sheahan (2012).

10. Zott, Amit, and Massa (2011).

11. Johnson, Christensen, and Kagerman (2008).

12. Johnson (2010).

13. Johnson, Christensen, and Kagerman (2008).

14. Morris, Schindehutte, and Allen (2005).

15. Ple, Lecocq, and Angot (2008).

16. Ple, Lecocq, and Angot (2008).

17. Chesbrough (2006).

18. Groonros and Rivald (2011).

19. Priem (2007).

20. Newton (2011).

21. Morris, Schindehutte, and Allen (2005).

22. Morris, Schindehutte, and Allen (2005).

23. Kim and Mauborgne (2005).

24. Priem (2007).

25. Blank and Dorf (2012).

26. Magretta (2002).

27. Shafer, Smith, and Linder (2005).

Chapter 3

1. Lai (1995).

2. Sundhar (2010).

3. Sundhar (2010).

4. Sundhar (2010).

5. Bomgar.com (2012).

6. Wong (2008).

7. Wong (2008).

8. Wong (2008).

9. Wong (2008).

10. Wong (2008).

11. Bettman (1979).

12. Woodruff (1997).

13. Woodruff (1997).

14. Huffman, Ratneshwar, and Mick (2000).

15. Rokeach (1968).

16. Rokeach (1968).

17. Huffman, Ratneshwar, and Mick (2000).

18. Marcus and Ruvolo (1989).

19. Marcus and Ruvolo (1989).

20. http://www.dapplebaby.com/our-story.html retrieved October 1, 2012.

21. Johnson, Christensen, and Hagerman (2008), p. 52.

22. Johnson, Christensen, and Kagerman (2008).

23. Nobel (2011).
24. Nobel (2011).
25. Nobel (2011).
26. Christopher et al. (1991).
27. Woodruff (1997).
28. Day and Crask (2000).
29. Day and Crask (2000).
30. Woodruff and Gardial (1996).
31. Zeithaml (1988).
32. Zeithaml (1987).
33. Lai (1995).
34. Rivald and Gronroos (1996).
35. Priem (2007).
36. Ratneshwar, Mick, and Huffman (2000).

Chapter 4

1. Nalley (2012).
2. Johnson, Christensen, and Kagerman (2008).
3. Morris, Schindehutte, and Allen (2008).
4. Magretta (2002).
5. Johnson, Christensen, and Kagerman (2008).
6. Johnson, Christensen, and Kagerman (2008).
7. MFJ Enterprises Website (2012).
8. Newton (2011).
9. Newton (2011), p. 21.
10. Newton (2011), p. 22.
11. Blank and Dorf (2012).
12. Schweizer (2005).
13. Schweizer (2005).

Chapter 5

1. Johnson, Christensen, and Kagermann (2008), p. 52.
2. Bansal (2012).
3. Mycoskie (2011).
4. Mycoskie (2011).
5. Mycoskie (2011).
6. Mycoskie (2011).
7. Murray and Wang (2011).
8. www.toms.com
9. Vitella (2011).
10. Schwartz (2011).
11. Cone Cause Evolution Study (2010).

12. Teece (2010), p. 188.
13. Bansal (2012).
14. Schweizer (2005).
15. Schweizer (2005).
16. Schweizer (2005).
17. Shah (2011).
18. Poulos (2012).
19. Karmini and Wright (2011).
20. Mainwaring (2010).
21. www.toms.com
22. Aakers (2012).
23. Aaker (2012).
24. Aaker (2012).
25. Q&A: Blake Mycoskie (2011).
26. Teece (2010).
27. Reich (2012).

Chapter 6

1. Ho (2006).
2. Blau (1964).
3. Liedtke (2011).
4. Liedtke (2012).
5. Hamel (2000).
6. Shafer, Smith and Linder (2005).
7. Shafer, Smith and Linder (2005).
8. Cheredar (2011).
9. Ludwig (2011)
10. Wilson and Crawford (2012).
11. Hoffman (2009).
12. Chesbrough (2010).
13. Gustin (2011).
14. Gustin (2011).
15. Wingfield and Stelter (2011).
16. Wingfield and Stelter (2011).
17. Wingfield and Stelter (2011).
18. Ple, Lecocq and Angot (2010).
19. Ple, Lecocq and Angot (2012).

Chapter 7

1. Orley (2012).
2. Fairchild (2012).
3. Levinson (2012).

4. Orley (2012).
5. Binkley (2011).
6. Hyman (2012).
7. Chatzki (2010).
8. Orley (2012).
9. Levinson (2012).
10. Levinson (2012).
11. Levinson (2012).
12. Orley (2012).
13. Chatzki (2010).
14. Lapowski (2012).
15. Lapowski (2012).
16. Binkley (2011).
17. Wahba (2011).
18. Roush (2010).
19. Ebbert (2012).
20. Binkley (2011).
21. Binkley (2011).
22. Binkley (2011).
23. Binkley (2011).
24. Orley (2012).
25. Wortham (2009).
26. Fleiss (2012).
27. Fleiss (2012).
28. Ballard (2012).
29. Del Castillo (2012).
30. Tungez (2011).
31. Tungez (2011).
32. Tungez (2011).
33. Walsh (2011).
34. Fairchild (2012).
35. Tungez (2011).
36. Botsman and Rogers (2010).
37. Levinson (2012).

Chapter 8

1. Ashkenas (2012).
2. Teece (2010).
3. Morris, Schindehutte, and Allen (2005).
4. Morris, Schindehutte, and Allen (2005).
5. Johnson, Christensen, and Kagerman (2008).
6. J.C. Penney.com (2012).

7. Tibbetts (1999).
8. Poggi (2012).
9. Lewis (2011).
10. Lewis (2011).
11. Lewis (2011).
12. Department stores Industry Report (2012).
13. Berk (2012).
14. Lauchheimer (2012).
15. Lauchheimer (2012).
16. Brugger (2012).
17. Chernev (2012).
18. Gallo (2012).
19. Gallo (2012).
20. Berk (2012).
21. Brown (2012).
22. Berk (2012).
23. Chernev (2012).
24. Moore (2012).
25. Coleman-Lochner (2012).
26. Brown (2012).
27. Brown (2012).
28. Loeb (2012).
29. McIntyre (2012).
30. Ries (2012).
31. Kalb (2012).
32. Bhasin (2012).
33. Askenas (2012).
34. Chernev (2012).
35. Chernev (2012).

Chapter 9

1. Zott and Amit (2008).
2. Teece (2010), p. 190.
3. Johnson, Christensen, and Kagerman (2008).
4. Chesbrough (2010).
5. Gronroos and Ravald (2011).
6. Hamel (2000).
7. Teece (2010).
8. Teece (2010).
9. Johnson, Christensen, and Kagerman (2008).

10. Morris, Schindehutte, and Allen (2005).
11. Morris, Schindehutte, and Allen (2005).

Appendix A

1. Weiss and Mehrotra (2001).
2. Lang (2012).
3. Junnarkar (1999).

Appendix B

1. 100 Auction Sites: 28 Leading Online Marketplaces. http://www.100auctionsites
.com/online-marketplaces.php.

References

Aaker, D. (2012). Win the brand relevance battle and then build competitor barriers. *California Management Review 54*(2), 43–57.

Afuah, A., & Tucci, C. (2001). *Internet Business Models and Strategies*. Boston, MA: McGraw Hill Irwin.

Argyris, C., & Schon, D. (1978). *Organizational learning: A theory of action perspective*. Reading, MA: Addison Wesley.

Ashkenas, R. (2012, Oct. 2). *Kill your business model before it kills you*. Harvard Business Review Online. Retrieved October 2, 2012, http://blogs.hbr.org /ashkenas/2012/10/kill-your-business-model-befor.html

Baden-Fuller & Morgan (2010). Business models as models. *Long Range Planning 43*, 156–171.

Ballard, M. (2012, Oct. 9). *Rent the Runway chooses Maxymizer to optimize its online experience*. EIN News, Retrieved, October 9, 2012, http://world .einnews.com/pr_news/83112484/rent-the-runway-chooses-maxymiser-to -optimize-the-online-customer-experience

Bansal, S. (2012). *Shopping for a better world*. New York Times Opinion Page, Retrieved May 9, 2012, http://opinionator.blogs.nytimes.com/2012/05/09 /shopping-for-a-better-world/

Berk, C. C. (2012). *Is J.C. Penney backpedaling from its pricing strategy?* CNBC .com. Retrieved May 30, 2012, http://www.cnbc.com/id/47617890/Is _JCPenney_Backpedaling_From_Its_Pricing_Strategy

Bettman, J. R. (1979). *An Information Processing Theory of Consumer Choice*. Reading, MA: Addison-Wesley Publishing Co.

Bhasin, K. (2012*). J.C. Penney broke a sacrad covenant and now it's paying for it*. Business Insider Retail. Retrieved October 5, 2012, http://www .businessinsider.com/jcpenney-ron-johnson-turnaround-trust-2012-10

Binkley, C. (2011). *Fashion 101: Rent the Runway targets students*. Wall Street Journal Online. Retrieved April 7, 2011, http://online.wsj.com/article/SB10 0014240527487038063045762449952860660370.html

Blank, S., & Dorf, B. (2012). *The Start-up Owner's Manual: The step by step guide for building a great company*. Peschadaro, CA: K&S Ranch Publishing Division.

Blau, P. (1964). *Exchange and Power in Social Life*. New York: Wiley.

Bomgar.com (2012).

Botsman, R., & Rogers, R. (2010). *What's Mine is Yours: The Rise of Collaborative Consumption*. Harper Collins.

Brown, A. (2012). *J.C. Penney's Turnaround goes the wrong way: Quarterly loss wider than expected*. Forbes. http://www.forbes.com/sites/abrambrown/2012/08/10 /j-c-penney-sees-greater-than-expected-quarterly-loss/

Brugger, T. (2012). *Have an opinion on J.C. Penney: Join the club*. Daily Finance. http://www.dailyfinance.com/2012/09/21/have-an-opinion-on-jc-penney -join-the-club/

Casadesus-Masanell, R., & Ricart, J. E. (2011, January). How to design a winning business model. *Harvard Business Review*, 100–107.

Chatzki, J. (2010). *Entrepreneur Friday: Rent the Runway*. JeanChatsky's Blog, Retrieved October 1, 2012. http://www.jeanchatzky.com/homepage /entrepreneur-friday-rent-the-runway/

Cheredar, T. (2011). *How Netflix dropped the ball by ignoring its customers*. Venturebeat.com, Retrieved October 7, 2011. http://venturebeat.com /2011/10/27/netflix-dropped-the-ball/

Chernev, A. (2012). *Two Questions haunting J.C. Penney*, Bloomberg Businessweek http://www.businessweek.com/articles/2012-08-13/two-questions- haunting-j-dot-c-dot-penney

Chesbrough, H.W. (2010). Business model innovation: Opportunities and Barriers. *Long Range Planning 43*, 354–363.

Coleman-Lochner, L. (2012). *J.C. Penney Falls after Francis leaves amid strategy flop*. Bloomberg.com. http://www.bloomberg.com/news/2012-06-18/j-c-penney -says-ceo-to-run-marketing-as-francis-leaves.html

Cone Cause Evolution Study (2010). Cone LLC, Boston, MA. http://www .coneinc.com/whatdoyoustandfor

Costello, A. (2012). *TOMS Shoes: A closer look*. Tiny Spark, Retrieved October 9, 2012, http://www.tinyspark.org/podcasts/toms-shoes/

Dapplebaby.com website http://www.dapplebaby.com/our-story.html. Retrieved October 12, 2012.

Day, E., & Crask, M. R. (2000). Value Assessment: The Antecedent of Customer Satisfaction. *Journal of Consumer Satisfaction, Dissatisfaction and Complaining Behavior 13*, 52–60.

Del Castillo (2012). *In fashion, the human touch beats algorithms*. Upstart Business Journal. http://upstart.bizjournals.com/entrepreneurs/hot-shots/2012/05/21 /rent-the-runway-uses-social-media-to-fit-couture-clothes.html?page=all

Dendukuri, R. (2010). http://www.scribd.com/doc/40684328/Netflix-%E2%80% 93-Strategic-Marketing-Plan

Department Store Industry Report (2012). *High Beam Business Report*. http: //business.highbeam.com/industry-reports/retail/department-stores.

Ebbert, J. (2012). *One Kings Lane and RTR take the stage at NRF Show*. Ad Exchanger, Retrieved January 17, 2012, http://www.adexchanger.com /advertiser/nrf-one-kings-lane-rent-the-runway/

Fairchild, C. (2012). *The rental generation sees no point in buying.* Bloomberg Businessweek Online, Retrieved August 9, 2012, http://www.businessweek.com/articles/2012-08-09/the-rental-generation-sees-no-point-in-buying#p2

Fleiss, J. (2012). *Best Advice I ever got.*. Retrieved Sept. 10, 2012, Inc.com. http://www.inc.com/young-entrepreneur-council/best-advice-i-ever-got-jennifer-fleiss.html

Gallo, C. (2012). *Five reasons why J.C. Penney's Ron Johnson will reinvent retail again.* Forbes. http://www.forbes.com/sites/carminegallo/2012/09/20/5-reasons-why-j-c-penneys-ron-johnson-will-reinvent-retail-again/

Gray, S. (2008). Aldi: A grocer for the recession. Retrieved October 28, 2008, http://www.time.com/time/nation/article/0,8599,1854348,00.html

Gronroos, C. & Rivald, A. (2011). Service as business logic: Implications for value creation and marketing. *Journal of Service Management 22*(1): 5–22.

Gustin, S. (2011). *Netflix profit up 88% but shares fall 5%.* Wired, Retrieved April 25, 2011, http://www.wired.com/business/2011/04/netflix-profit-up/

Hamel, G. (2000). *Leading the Revolution.* New York: Penguin.

Handfield, R. (2006). *A brief history of outsourcing.* Retrieved June 29, 2012, http://scm.ncsu.edu/scm-articles/article/a-brief-history-of-outsourcing

Huffman, C., Ratneshwar, S., & Mick, D. G. (2000). Consumer goal structures and goal determination processes: An integrative framework. In Ratneshwar, S., Mick, D.G., and Huff man, C. (Eds.), *The why of consumption: Contemporary perspectives on consumer motives, goals and desires,* pp. 1–9. London and New York: Routledge.

Ho, C. (2006). Exchange-based value creation system for network relationships. *The Journal of American Academy of Business 9*(1), 202–209.

Hoffman, H. (2009). *Netflix awards $1 million for outdoing Cinemax.* c/Net, Retrieved September 21, 2009, http://news.cnet.com/8301-13515_3-10357807-26.html

Holloway, S. S., & Sebastio, H. J. (2010). The role of business model innovation in the emergence of markets: A missing dimension of entrepreneurial strategy. *Journal of Strategic Innovation and Sustainability 6*(4), 86–100.

J.C. Penney.com website. http://www.jcpenney.net/Our-Old-Company/About-jcpenney/Our-History.aspx

Jenn Hyman. (2012). How to build buzz for your brand. Retrieved July 19, 2012, http://fashionista.com/2012/07/fashionpreneur-with-rent-the-runways-jenn-hyman-how-to-build-buzz-for-your-brand/

Johnson, M. W. (2010). *Seizing the white space: Business model innovation for growth and renewal.* Boston, MA: Harvard Business Press.

Johnson, M. W., Christensen, C. M., & Kagermann, H. (2008). Reinventing your business model. Harvard *Business Review 86*(12), 50–59.

Junnarkar, S. (1999). *Pay-per-use app market blooming, benefits unclear.* Cnet, Retrieved June 4, 1999, http://news.cnet.com/2100-1001-226705.html&st.ne.fd.gif.k

Kalb, I. (2012). J.C. Penney's entire rebranding was way off. Business Insider. Retrieved May 17, 2012, http://www.businessinsider.com/earth-to-jcp -inside-out-thinking-rarely-works-2012-5

Karmini, N. & Wright, S. (2011). Nike faces new worker abuse claims. The Jakarta Post. Retrieved July 13, 2011, http://www.thejakartapost.com /news/2011/07/13/nike-faces-new-worker-abuse-claims.html

Keen, P. & Qureshi, S. (2006). Organizational Transformation through business models: A framework for business model design. Proceedings of the 39th Hawaii Conference on System Sciences, 1–10.

Kim, C.W. & Mauborgne, R. (2005). *Blue Ocean Strategy: How to Create Uncontested Market Space and Make the Competition Irrelevant.* Boston, MA: Harvard Business School Press.

Kraemer, D. & Sharma (2009). One laptop per child: Vision vs. reality. *Communications of the ACM 52*(6), 66–73.

Lai, A. W. (1995). Consumer values, product benefits, and customer value: A consumption behavior approach. *Advances in Consumer Research 22*, 381–388.

Lang, B. (2012). *Finally, Good News for Newspapers: Paywalls Are Paying Off.* The Wrap, Retrieved May 2, 2012, http://www.thewrap.com/media/column-post /paywalls-growing-dominance-reflected-newspaper-circulation-increases-38266.

Lapowski, I. (2012). *The way I work, Jennifer Hyman: Rent the Runway.* Inc. Magazine, Retrieved January 24, 2012, http://www.inc.com/magazine/201202 /the-way-i-work-jennifer-hyman-rent-the-runway.html

Lauchheimer, D. (2012). *JC Penney: Tremendous upside with an internal hedge. Seeking Alpha.* Retrieved June 6, 2012. http://seekingalpha.com /article/639911-j-c-penney-tremendous-upside-with-an-internal-hedge.

Lee, K. (2012). *Warby Parker's honest brand voice.* Forbes Online, Retrieved September 19, 2012. http://www.forbes.com/sites/katelee/2012/09/19 /warby-parkers-honest-brand-voice/

Levinson, P. (2012). Rent the Runway's HBS founders and VCs create a Cinderella story. The Harbus Online, Retrieved February 12, 2012. http://www.harbus. org/2012/rent-the-runway/

Lewis, R. (2011). *Macy's: The Biggest and last department store standing? Or an emerging new model.* The Robin Report. Retrieved November 27, 2011, http:// therobinreport.com/macys-the-biggest-and-last-department-store-standing -or-an-emerging-new-model/

Liedtke, M. (2011). *Netflix customer rebellion pummels shares.* Startribune Business, Retrieved October 24, 2011, http://www.startribune.com /business/132503438.html?refer=y

Liedtke, M. (2012). *Netflix stock still struggling one year after subscription price hike.* Huffington Post, Retrieved July 13, 2012, http://www.huffingtonpost .com/2012/07/13/netflix-stock_n_1672153.html

Linder, J. & S. Cantrell (2000). *Changing business models: Surveying the landscape*, Accenture Institute for Strategic Change. http://www.accenture.com/NR /rdonlyres/0DE8F2BE-5522-414C-8E1B-E19CF...

Loeb, W. (2012). *J.C. Penney's Ron Johnson had an epiphany, let's see if it works.* Forbes.com. http://www.forbes.com/sites/walterloeb/2012/04/26/j-c-penneys -ron-johnson-had-an-epiphany/

Ludwig, S. (2011). Netflix raises plan prices by 60%, with 4100 negative comments and counting. http://venturebeat.com/2011/07/12/netflix-raises -plan-prices-by-60-with-4100-negative-comments-and-counting/

Magretta, J. (2002). Why Business Models Matter. *Harvard Business Review* *80*(5), 3–8.

Markus, H. & Ruvolo, A. (1989). Possible selves: Personalized representations of goals. In L.A. Pervin (ed.), *Goal concepts in personality and social psychology* (pp. 211–241). Hillsdale, N.J.: Erlbaum.

McIntyre, D. A. (2012). Enthusiasm about JC Penney Turnaround ends. 24/7 Wall St. Morning newsletter. http://247wallst.com/2012/05/08/enthusiasm -about-a-jcpenney-turnaround-ends/

Mainwaring, S. (2010). *TOMS vs. BOBS: How Skechers shot themselves in the foot.* Fast Company Retrieved October 21, 2010. http://www.fastcompany. com/1696887/toms-vs-bobs-how-skechers-shot-themselves-foot

MFJ Enterprises Website http://www.mfjenterprises.com/about_mfj.php, Retrieved September 7, 2012.

Moore, S. (2012). *Internet Retailer: JC Penney treads water on the web.* Internet Retailer. http://www.internetretailer.com/mobile/2012/02/24/jc-penney-treads -water-web

Morin, P. (2011). *11 Things Venture Capitalists Look For.* Retrieved August 21. http://www.companyfounder.com/2011/08/11-things-venture-capital -investors-look-for/

Morris, M., Schindehutte, M., & Allen, J. (2005). The entrepreneur's business model: Toward a unified perspective. *Journal of Business Research* *58*, 726–735.

Murray, M. & Wang, J. (2011). *Person of the week: TOMS Shoe founder Blake Mycoskie.* ABC News Online, Retreived April 8, 2011. http://abcnews .go.com/International/PersonOfWeek/person-week-toms-shoes-founder -blake-mycoskie/story?id=13331473#.UHSoK65YWSp

Mycoskie (2011). *Blake Mycoskie, How I Did It: The TOMS Story*, Retrieved September 19, 2011, http://www.secondact.com/2011/09/how-i-did-it-the-toms-story/

Nalley, S. (2012). Amateur Radio Company marks 40th anniversary. Starkville Daily News. Retrieved October 4, 2012.

Newton, D. B. (2011). *Business Models for Entrepreneurial Ventures: Developing Sound Metrics for Long-Term Success.* Santa Barbara, CA: E3 Free Market Press.

Nobel, C. (2011). *Clay Christensen's Milkshake Marketing. Working Knowledge: The Thinking That Leads.* Retrieved on February 14, 2011, http://hbswk.hbs.edu/item/6496.html

Orley, A. (2012). *Rent the Runway buys into social media.* CNBC Small Business, Retrieved August 16, 2012. http://www.cnbc.com/id/48687830/Rent_the_Runway_Buys_Into_Social_Media

Osterwalder, A., Pigneur, Y., & Tucci, C. L. (2005). Clarifying business models: Origins, present, and future of the concept. *Communications of AIS 16*(1).

Ple, Lecocq & Angot (2010). Customer-integrated business models: A theoretical framework. *M@n@gement 13*(4), 226–265.

Poggi, J. (2012). *Retailers look to department stores for salvation.* Advertising Age Retrieved March 19, 2012. http://adage.com/article/news/retailers-department-store-salvation/233366/

Porter, M. (1996). What is strategy? *Harvard Business Review*, November–December, 61–78.

Poulos, J. (2012). *Toms shoes: A Doomed vanity project*, Forbes. Retreived April 11, 2012, http://www.forbes.com/sites/jamespoulos/2012/04/11/toms-shoes-a-doomed-vanity-project/

Priem, R. L. (2007). A consumer perspective on value creation. *Academy of Management Review 22*(1), 219–235.

Q&A: Blake Mycoskie (2012). *360 Research*, Steelcase, Issue 58, Retrieved October 1, 2011. http://360.steelcase.com/articles/q-a-blake-mycoskie/

Rappa, M. (2001). *Managing the digital enterprise: Business models on the Web.* http://digitalenterprise.org/models/models.html

Reich, R. (2012). *The problem isn't outsourcing. It's that the prosperity of big business has become disconnected from the well-being of most Americans.* Retrieved July 8, 2012, http://robertreich.org/post/27527895909

Ries, A. (2012). *What J.C. Penney should have done—and still can do—to make reinvention work.* Ad Age Blogs. Retrieved August 7, 2012, http://adage.com/article/al-ries/al-ries-prescription-fix-jc-penney-retail-reinvention/236564/

Rivald, A. & Gronroos, C. (1996). The value concept and relationship marketing. *European Journal of Marketing 30*(2), 19–30.

Rokeach, M. (1968). Beliefs, attitudes and values: A theory of organization and change. San Fransisco: Jossey-Bass.

Roush, W. (2010). *Subscription model turns RTR into real "Dressflix."* http://www.xconomy.com/boston/2010/01/08/subscription-model-turns-rent-the-runway-into-a-real-dressflix/

Sarasvathy, S. D. & Dew, N. (2005). New market creation through transformation. *Journal of Evolutionary Economics 15*, 533–565.

Schwartz, A. (2011). *TOMS Shoes CEO Blake Mycoskie on social entrepreneurship, telling stories, and his new book*. Fast Company, Retrieved September 6, 2011. http://www.fastcompany.com/1776334/toms-shoes-ceo-blake-mycoskie -social-entrepreneurship-telling-stories-and-his-new-book

Shah, A. (2011). The TOMS Development Model. *Values & Capitalism*. 15 Jun. Online blog. Retrieved April 4, 2012. http://www.valuesandcapitalism.com /dialogue/poverty/TOMS-development-model

Shafer, S. M., Smith, H. J., & Linder, J. C. (2005). The power of business models. *Business Horizons 48*(3), 199–207.

Schweizer, L. (2005). Concept and evolution of business models. Journal of General Management, 31(2), 37–56.

heahan, K. (2012). Three Types of Business Models. In Small Business (by Demand Media), associated with the Houston Chronicle. http://smallbusiness.chron. com/three-types-business-models-838.html (Retrieved 9/24, 2012).

Stähler, P. (2012). The strange business of airlines. Business Model Innovation Blog. http://blog.business-model-innovation.com/2012/05/strange_business _models_of_airlines/

Sundhar, S. (2010). Turning an idea into $30M a year: Joel Bomgar CEO. Fins Technology Career Strategies, Retrieved November 23, 2010. http://it-jobs .fins.com/Articles/SB129020569234259217/Turning-An-Idea-into-30M-a -Year-Joel-Bomgar-CEO

Teece, D. J. (2007). How to capture value from innovation: Shaping intellectual property and industry architecture. *California Management Review 50*(1), 278–296.

Teece, D.J. (2010). Business models, business strategy and innovation. *Long Range Planning 43*, 172–194.

Thau, B. (2012). *JCP's CEO: Falling sales and rising cynics won't stop the transformation.* Investor Center. Retrieved October 3, 2012, http://www.dailyfinance.com/2012 /10/03/jcps-ceo-falling-sales-and-rising-cynics-wont-stop-the-transf/

Tibbetts, O. L. (1999). *The Spiritual Journey of J. C. Penney,* New York and London: Routledge Books.

Timmers, P. (1998). Business models for electronic markets. *Electronic Markets 8*(2), 3–8.

Tom's Shoes Website, Corporate Responsibility at Toms. Retrieved October 1, 2012, http://www.toms.com/eyewear/corporate-responsibility/

Tunguz, T. (2011). *How collaborative consumption is transforming startups.* MIT Entrepreneurship Review, Retreived April 17, 2011. http://www .huffingtonpost.com/mit-entrepreneurship-review/peertopeer-startups-are -e_b_837144.html

Usher, R. & Bryant, I. (1989). *Adult Education as Theory, Practice and Research.* London: Routledge, p. 87

Vitella, C. (2011). *Why TOMS Shoes Seem Like Charity, Rumination Avenue,* Retrieved May 3, 2011. http://ruminationavenue.com/2011/05/03/why-toms-shoes-pose-as-charity/

Wahba (2011). *Reuters Summit—Rent the Runway gets $15 M from KPCB,* Retrieved May 23, 2011. http://uk.reuters.com/article/2011/05/23/idUKN2312023520110523

Walsh, B. (2011) *Ten ideas that will change the world: Today's smart choice, don't own. Share.* Time online. Retrieved May 17, 2011. http://www.collaborativeconsumption.com/buzz-and-press/Today%20s%20Smart%20Choice%3A%20Don%20t%20Own.%20Share%20-%2010%20Ideas%20That%20Will%20Change%20the%20World%20-%20TIME.pdf

Weiss & Mehrotra (2001). Online Dynamic Pricing: Efficiency, Equity and the Future E-Commerce. Virginia *Journal of Law and Technology.*

Wilson, T. & Crawford, S. (2012). *How Netflix works. How Stuff Works* Retrieved September 30, 2012, http://electronics.howstuffworks.com/netflix.htm

Wingfield, N. & Stelter, B. (2011). *How Netflix lost 800,000 members and goodwill.* New York Times Technology Online, Retrieved October 24, 2011. http://www.nytimes.com/2011/10/25/technology/netflix-lost-800000-members-with-price-rise-and-split-plan.html

Wong, W. (2008, December). Taking control. *Baseline Magazine,* 31–32.

Wong, W. (2011). *Investors want in on Groupon deal.* Chicago Tribune Business Online. Retrieved November 5, 2011.

Woodruff, R. B. (1997, March 1). Customer Value: The Next Source for Competitive Advantage. *Journal of the Academy of Marketing Science,* pp. 139–153. Spring.

Woodruff, R. B. & Gardial, S. F. (1996). *Know your customer: New approaches to understanding customer value and satisfaction.* Reading, MA: Addison Wesley Publishing Co.

Wortham, J. (2009). *A Netflix model for haute couture.* New York Times Technology, Retrieved November 8, 2009. http://www.nytimes.com/2009/11/09/technology/09runway.html?_r=0

Zeithaml, V. (1987). *Defining and Relating Price, Perceived Quality, and Perceived Value.* Report 87–101, Cambridge, MA: Marketing Science Institute.

Zeithaml, V. (1988). Consumer perceptions of price, quality and value: A means-end model and synthesis of evidence. *Journal of Marketing 52,* 2–22.

Zott, C. & Amit, R. (2008). The fit between product market strategy and business model: Implications for firm performance, *Strategic Management Journal 29,* 1–26.

Zott, C., Amit, R., & Massa, L. (2011). The business model: Recent developments and future research. *Journal of Management 37,* 1019–1042.

Index

A
Adaptive business model
    customer and firm relationship, 5–6
    customer attitudes and behaviors, 23
    foundation and differentiators, 22
    Rent the Runway (RTR), 73–74
    revenues, 23
    TOMS shoes, 58–59
    value exchange relationship, 22

B
Bomgar box
    benefits and sacrifices
        Bomgar's multiplatform
            capability, 35
        costs, 34
        deliverables, 36–37
        emotional outcomes, 33
        levels of drivers, 35
        physical outcomes, 33
        social outcomes, 33
        trade-offs, 34
        use-value, 33
    Bomgar, Joel
        appliance-based products, 28
        HMHP Company, 28–29
        part-time IT support
            representative, 27
        remote-administration tool, 29
        software promotion, 28
    customer value hierarchy
        economic and social goals, 30
        long-term goals and
            purposes, 30–31
        problem solving, 31–33
        product costs and benefits, 29
        Woodruff's hierarchy, 29–30

Business models. *See also specific*
        business models
    adaptability, 10
    agreement, 2
    business-model-in-use, 94
    business outsourcing, 13
    collaborative consumption, 101
    commodity, 2
    conceptual tool, 93–94
    costs and benefits, 97–98
    customers, 17
        cocreation, 101
        goals and aspirations, 97
        relationship, 2
        value proposition, 3, 99–100
    definition, 3, 15
    deliverables, 98–99
    dynamic, 102
    e-business, 14
    elements, 16
    entrepreneur, 16–17
    feasibility, 10
    firm and customers relationship, 17
    Internet, 101
    lenses, 95–96
        adaptive business model (*see*
            Adaptive business model)
        differentiated business model
            (*see* Differentiated
            business model)
        foundation level business model
            (*see* Foundation business
            model)
        implementation, 24–25
    partnerships, 103
    problem solving, 96–97
    reinvestment, 101

Ron Ashkenas's blog, 79
strategic analysis, 102
strategic circumstances, 80
strategic thinking, 103
  vs. strategy, 6–8
sustainability, 10, 102
trade-offs, 98
value exchange relationship, 8–9
vertically integrated firms, 101
viability, 10, 79
Business outsourcing, 13

C
Crowd-sourcing algorithm, 65
Customer value proposition, 3, 5, 16, 18
  Ham radio company,
    MFJ Enterprises, 43
  J.C. Penney store, 87
  Rent the Runway (RTR), 72–73
  TOMS shoes, 53

D
Differentiated business model
  Blue Ocean strategy, 22
  business model foundation
    separation, 21
  customer expectation, 22
  customer value proposition, 5
  ham radio company,
    MFJ Enterprises
    company website, 46
    hamfests, 46
    innovation capabilities, 45
    integrated business
      models, 46–47
    value proposition, 46
  J.C. Penney store
    customer value proposition, 87
    key processes, 86–87
    key resources, 85–86
    leadership and vision, 84–85
    profit margin, 87
  Netflix, value exchange
    agreement, 64–65
  Rent the Runway (RTR)
    customer value proposition, 72–73
    key processes, 71–72
    key resources, 71

  leadership and vision, 70–71
  profit formula, 72
  sustainable competitive
    advantage, 20
  TOMS shoes
    customer value proposition, 53
    firm leadership and
      logic, 53–54
    key resources and
      processes, 51–52
    profit margin, 52–53
    uniqueness, 5
Dynamic business model, 102

E
e-Business models, 14

F
Foundation business model
  customer value proposition, 18
  definition, 5
  ham radio company (*see* Ham radio
    company, MFJ Enterprises)
  key resources and processes, 18–19
  profit formula, 19–20
  resources and develop
    processes, 17

H
Ham radio company,
  MFJ Enterprises
  differentiators
    company website, 46
    hamfests, 46
    innovation capabilities, 45
    integrated business
      models, 46–47
    value proposition, 46
  foundation business model
    customer value proposition, 43
    elements, 40–41
    feasibility, 43–44
    firm aspirations and goals, 41
    hypothesis testing, 43
    key processes, 42
    key resources, 42
    profit formula, 42–43
    viability, 44–45

Jue, Martin
    ham number, K5FLU, 39
    hobby, 46
    Morse code, 39
    personality and background, 46
    vertical integration, 47

J
J.C. Penney store
    background, 81
    department stores rise and fall
        competitors, 82
        discounting techniques, 83
        mass merchants, 83
        online stores, 83
        palaces of consumption, 82
        T.J. Maxx and Ross Stores, 83
        Walmart, 83–84
    differentiated business model
        customer value proposition, 87
        key processes, 86–87
        key resources, 85–86
        leadership and vision, 84–85
        profit margin, 87
    model changes
        business opportunities, 91
        competitor disruption, 90
        consumers education, 92
        fair-and-square pricing policy, 91
        focused value proposition, 90
        fundamental change, 91
        hypothesis testing, 91
        negative influences, 90
        staffing levels, 90
        store brands, 90
    strategic repositioning, 84
    value exchange agreement, 88–89

K
Key processes, 16, 18–19
    ham radio company,
        MFJ Enterprises, 42
    J.C. Penney store, 86–87
    Netflix, value exchange
        agreement, 63
    Rent the Runway (RTR), 71–72
    TOMS shoes, 51–52
Key resources, 16, 18–19

ham radio company,
    MFJ Enterprises, 42
J.C. Penney store, 85–86
Netflix, value exchange
    agreement, 63
Rent the Runway (RTR), 71
TOMS shoes, 51–52

N
Netflix, value exchange agreement
    logic and internal consistency, 62
    relationship, 61–62
    reputation and credibility, 63
    streaming business, 62
    unlimited DVDs by mail, 61–62
    value network, 62
    value propositions, 63
    winning model vs. changes
        crowd-sourcing algorithm, 65
        customer decisions, 66
        differentiated business model
            lens, 64–65
        film library, 63
        key processes, 63
        key resources, 63
        profit margin, 64
        social community, 66
        video streaming, 64
Nike company, 55

M
MFJ Enterprises. See Ham radio
        company, MFJ Enterprises

O
Orchestrator model, 54–56

P
Philanthropic Capitalism, 59
Profit formula, 16, 19–20
    ham radio company,
        MFJ Enterprises, 42–43
    Rent the Runway (RTR), 72
Profit margin
    J.C. Penney store, 87
    Netflix, value exchange
        agreement, 64
    TOMS shoes, 52–53

R
Rent the Runway (RTR)
  adaptive business
    model, 73–74
  bridal wear, 78
  collaborative consumption, 76–77
  competitors, 78
  customer behavior, 69
  customer feedback, 77
  customer goals and aspirations, 73
  customer relationships, 74–75
  differentiated business model
    customer value proposition, 72–73
    key processes, 71–72
    key resources, 71
    leadership and vision, 70–71
    profit formula, 72
  emotional connection, 73
  free membership website, 69
  learning and adaptability, 77
  social network, 77
  socioeconomic groundswell, 77
  sustainability, 73–74

T
TOMS shoes
  adaptive business model, 58–59
  differentiated business model
    customer value proposition, 53
    firm leadership and logic, 53–54
    key resources and
      processes, 51–52
    profit margin, 52–53
  Mycoskie, Blake
    alpargata, 50
    The Amazing Race, 50
    buy-one give-one business
      model, 49
    company history, 51
    donation relied
      organization, 50
    other business, 50
  orchestrator model, 54–56
  Philanthropic Capitalism, 59
  sustainability, 56–57

V
Value exchange relationship, 8–9
Value exchange agreement
  J.C. Penney store, 88–89
  Netflix (*see* Netflix, value exchange
    agreement)

W
Woodruff's customer value
  hierarchy, 29–30

OTHER TITLES IN THE STRATEGIC MANAGEMENT COLLECTION

William Q. Judge, Old Dominion University, Collection Editor

- *Grow by Focusing on What Matters: Competitive Strategy in 3-Circles* by Joel E. Urbany and James H. Davis
- *Building Organizational Capacity for Change: The Leader's New Mandate* by William Q. Judge
- *Business Intelligence: Making Decisions Through Data Analytics* by Jerzy Surma
- *Designing the Networked Organization* by Ken Everett
- *Successful Organizational Transformation: The Five Critical Elements* by Marvin Washington, Stephen Hacker, and Marla Hacker
- *Top Management Teams: How to Be Effective Inside and Outside the Boardroom* by Annaloes M.L. Raes
- *The Family in Business: The Dynamics of the Family Owned Firm* by Bernard Liebowitz
- *A Stakeholder Approach to Issues Management* by Robert Boutilier
- *The Strategic Management of Higher Education Institutions: Serving Students as Customers for Institutional Growth* by Hamid Kazeroony
- *Managing for Ethical-Organizational Integrity: Principles and Processes for Promoting Good, Right, and Virtuous Conduct* by Abe Zakhem
- *Corporate Bankruptcy Fundamental Principles and Processes* by William J. Donoher
- *Learning Organizations: Turning Knowledge into Action* by Marcus Goncalves
- *Moral Leadership: A Transformative Model for Tomorrow's Leaders* by Cam Caldwell
- *Knowledge Management: The Death of Wisdom: Why Our Companies Have Lost It—and How They Can Get It Back* by Arnold Kransdorff
- *Intellectual Property in the Managerial Portfolio: Its Creation, Development, and Protection* by Thomas O'Connor
- *Strategy and Training: Making Skills a Competitive Advantage* by Philippe Korda
- *Business Models and Strategic Management: A New Integration* by Francine Newth

Announcing the Business Expert Press Digital Library

*Concise E-books Business Students Need for Classroom
and Research*

This book can also be purchased in an e-book collection by your library as

- a one-time purchase,
- that is owned forever,
- allows for simultaneous readers,
- has no restrictions on printing, and
- can be downloaded as PDFs from within the library community.

Our digital library collections are a great solution to beat the rising cost of textbooks. e-books can be loaded into their course management systems or onto student's e-book readers.

The **Business Expert Press** digital libraries are very affordable, with no obligation to buy in future years. For more information, please visit **www.businessexpertpress.com/librarians**. To set up a trial in the United States, please contact **Adam Chesler** at *adam.chesler@businessexpertpress .com* for all other regions, contact **Nicole Lee** at *nicole.lee@igroupnet.com*.